One-Armed Bandit

Shocking True Tales from the Repo Biz

by

Lefty

DORRANCE PUBLISHING CO., INC.
PITTSBURGH, PENNSYLVANIA 15222

All Rights Reserved
Copyright © 2009 by Lefty
No part of this book may be reproduced or transmitted
in any form or by any means, electronic or mechanical,
including photocopying, recording, or by any information
storage and retrieval system without permission in
writing from the publisher.

ISBN: 978-1-4349-0132-3
Library of Congress Control Number: 2008911223

Printed in the United States of America

First Printing

For more information or to order additional books, please contact:
Dorrance Publishing Co., Inc.
701 Smithfield Street
Pittsburgh, Pennsylvania 15222
U.S.A.
1-800-788-7654
www.dorrancebookstore.com

Dedication

I would like to dedicate this first book to my children: Michael, Kayla, and Kelsey. Also, a special thanks to the Los Angeles Police Department and the Los Angeles County Sheriffs Department, for rescuing me in my many times of need.

Contents

Foreword vii
Introduction ix
About the Author xi

The Three Hundred-Pound Lap Dance 1
    Once in a while, a customer gets really creative when trying to stop me. This woman tries using her best *asset*.

"Balls-Out" in San Pedro 5
    This country bumpkin "goes for the gold" in what should be a new Olympic event.

Crackhead Surprise! 13
    Being exposed to the dangers of the streets all alone every night does eventually catch up to me, when here I fight for my life with infuriating anger.

Doggie Do-Rite 19
    They don't call him man's best friend for nothing. But not when the family pet "costs you the family car."

G-Ma and the Gang-Stas 24
    After being confronted in a blind alley, I was surprised to find myself in the deadly grasp of their leader, an *eighty-year-old woman!*

"We're Gonna Die" 29
    A *frantic driver adds to the drama, as we find ourselves in a very serious* near-death experience!

Laying and Lying..36
    The Academy Awards are coming up, as this unpolished actor tries to call my bluff in a performance that *just can't be missed!*

The School Bully..45
    Once again I find myself at the mercy of every schoolboy's nightmare. But this time, I started it.

Taze the Puppet..52
    Intense fear turns to sarcastic humor when I'm able to use my quick wit in turning around a frightening situation.

Tommy's Lay-Down..61
    This showdown is mismatched when I find myself at gunpoint by the LAPD...on center stage!

Glossary..67

Foreword

In this long-continuing series of true-to-life events, I have put together a rather different way of looking at what is *one* of the most exciting jobs in America today: auto repossession!

The interesting way I am going to describe the following actual events may seem a bit twisted at times, but having lasted twenty years in such a stressful line of work, I had to learn some very important tools in being able to survive out there on the mean streets of Los Angeles. And without a doubt, the most essential thing a guy has to have to do this crazy job is an endless amount of courage!

There has been a few television documentaries, and also a couple short series, about the repossession and bounty hunter industry, but there is no *Hollywood reenactment or actual live footage* that can capture the *shear terror one can feel* when getting a limb torn off by a crazy, psychotic individual when the love of his life is being taken from him *right before his eyes*. But I can!

My name is Lefty, and *I am an amputee.*

No, I did not get my arm ripped off by a customer while taking his car. I lost it in a tree accident, but I had you going, didn't I?

The reason the stories compiled in this collection have been written in such a humorous fashion is not to disrespect or degrade the desperate person who is losing their car. The manner which these actual events are described is to show you a side of life that will help you in understanding that just having a sense of humor can get you through *just about anything!*

Trust me, at the time each of these extractions were taking place, the lack of tension I convey and use of sarcasm in describing each situation is replaced at the time by a thick, dark cloud of deadly desperation.

Just **being there** is the only way you can really understand how *tense* and *fast* things take place. And being an amputee happens to add another whole dimension to the each event just by default.

One-Armed Bandit is the title chosen for this series of stories I hope you will find not only entertaining in its original format but inspirational, and I hope it thus teaches you the fact that you can do *anything* if you put your mind to it!

Introduction

In the county of Los Angeles in 1985, there was a baby being born every thirty seconds, eight deaths an hour, an auto accident happening every ten to fifteen seconds, and an *auto repossession* every *eighteen minutes!*

Here in sunny southern California exists a paradise for those mid-westerners, East Coast survivors, and all the rest of the nation to follow their dream, by skipping out on their car payments and running out to Los Angeles, where the streets are lined with gold from the glitter of Hollywood. Unfortunately, many of those up-and-coming actors and actresses in their pursuit of happiness do not make it past the graveyard shift of Denny's.

But the local car lots do, in fact, see all that acting potential and finance them a really nice car to help "represent them" in the many important auditions they make on their "climb up that ladder to stardom." Once the new-found talent has signed on that dotted line to acquire that oh, so necessary set of wheels to get around LA, they have given the financial institution, who is carrying the contract for the dealer, permission to do whatever is necessary to recover (repo) the collateral (the car) once our new star is inconveniently between a series and their next commercial.

In the State of California, there is a certain agency that *must be involved*, if that collateral is to be picked up and brought back to the legal owner, once our proud driver "flakes out" on the payments. This picking-up process is what we like to call in financial terminology "adjusting the loan," and the one who does the actual adjusting of the loan is, who else, an *adjuster*. But seeing how his "job" has a lot more of a *physical presence* to it, we gave this agent of goodwill, this financial hero, the "most unpopular guy" in the neighborhood, that degrading tag of...the repo man! It's unfortunate that any person who has ever been overly delinquent on a car payment will never get the chance of *actually making "his" acquaintance*. And it's not because he is shy or that his busy schedule won't permit it. No, the reason you will most likely never meet that devil who takes away your livelihood is because he is *semi-invisible*. Yes, as rude as it seems, this elusive character is not any more interested in networking with you as you are with him. His *sole purpose in life* is to take away your only mode of transportation: the family car!

The following series of stories, which I have collectively called *One-Armed Bandit,* describes, in all fashionable detail, the extraordinary effort these "unfortunate victims of society" will put themselves through just to stop from having their car returned to the rightful owner. After you have immersed yourself in the reading of these *true stories* of what is sure to be a "reality check" in the desperate measures society has placed on human existence, you too will most likely not be able to go back to sleep once you, yourself, have been woken up by a *car alarm*. That nagging thought will keep you tossing and turning all night long...

Did I make the car payment?

About the Author

Lefty was conceived in a northern Michigan mental institution by two patients who happened to find love in such an awkward place where others only find misery and misfortune. At one year old, he was adopted by his caretakers, Audrey and Art Crain, and introduced into a loving family of two boys and two girls. He became the fifth (the sixth was a secret older brother, Bob, who was himself put up for adoption) child to take up the Crain name.

As each of the children became teenagers, they were no longer able to ignore the growing problem with their father's alcoholism. And being the youngest, Lefty was the last at home and unfortunately suffered the most.

After finding a way of escaping from the mental and physical abuse from his adopted father through drugs, Lefty was finally able to figure out how to break away and chase his dream of playing the drums. His father had begun calling the police on him, so he had to go out on his own.

The only way he was going be able to develop *his muse* was to run away from home. So at age sixteen, after quitting school only after one semester of tenth grade, Lefty moved in with a friend whose mother had just past away.

Together, with a few other unruly musicians in town, they took up the American Dream of starting a rock-n'-roll band, right there in the dead mother's bedroom.

The way he decided to deal with his home life with his parents became his misfortune, as his drug addiction became his main focus in life for the next twenty years. That was until he fully committed himself to "the program" in 1999.

At the age of twenty, Lefty received a letter from the State of Michigan informing him that his real mother wanted to meet him. So there in the wire-meshed caged windows of the state hospital did "Mikey" (as she called him), for the *first time ever, look into the eyes* of his natural mother, Joyce Scherzer Johnson.

The whole event, before and after, was so profound that a whole chapter could be written about it, and it would be "My Name Is Lefty and I Am Not Right."

The very next year, Lefty received another letter from the State of Michigan. But this time it was addressed from the Bureau of Indian and Family Affairs. It seemed he had enough Cherokee blood in him that his heritage was protected, and he earned the right to know his natural father's side of the family.

So in a tepee his Aunt June Soper lived in year 'round in the Traverse City State Park, Lefty met his wild and crazy roots!

After that meeting in 1978, Lefty decided since he was already "disowned" by his foster dad, it was only obvious that he take up the name of his birth parents. So he legally changed his name.

After continuing his career as a rock-n'-roll drummer, he moved to the LA area in 1980 and took on other jobs to subsidize his meager musician's income in the construction industry. He also found a new career as a tree trimmer in which he started his own company. But on November 11, 1984, Lefty found himself almost crushed to death when *at the hand* of the ex-lumberjack customer, a tree *he had just cut down* took an unexpected twist and...*pounded him into a concrete driveway!*

After waking up with *many* traumatic injuries, it was the fact that his *left arm* had to be amputated below the elbow that was the turning point in his life!

Lefty was still so very grateful just to be alive and was fortunate to not have broken his spirit along with the rest of his body. So as soon as he was able, and along with the support of his girlfriend and bandmates, he pulled himself up out of his wheelchair and got back *behind his drumset* and, to the surprise of all (including himself), developed a way to continue playing drums *with only one hand!*

His perseverance did not stop there, as his pool game improved to the point of him having to "play up" just to stay challenged.

But it was the love of rock-n'-roll that kept his drive alive as his band—Rager, at the time—began doing benefits for children who also found themselves and their families without insurance to cover their traumatic injuries. To show he didn't lose his sense of humor along with his limb, he instinctively took up the name of Lefty. In doing this, he let all the "lookey-lews" know, "Hey, I know I'm missing an arm, but I'm proud of it, so watch this!" Lefty saw the challenge in doing all the things normal guys do with two hands much more interesting with only one, so prosthetics were not part of the equation for him.

The amputation was done while he was without health insurance. So the incredible *rebuild* the doctors did of his elbow left him with a very thin layer of skin over a bone which, along with bleeding easily from simple ware, was way too painful, and the severed nerves were right near the surface, so just the weight of a prosthetic arm was unbearable. Besides, he thought the fake arm made him feel like a robot!

Not being one to just "lay down" and live off the State by drawing a disability check once a month, he unfortunately tried trimming trees but quickly came to the realization that his days of manual labor were over!

Most job descriptions are outlined for the use of both hands. That is why it was difficult to get past the liability factor when he sought out other lines of employment. The corporate world does not have the patience or the insurance coverage to accommodate a one-armed employee. But Lefty is so original with his ideas and along with being mechanically inclined, his work performance moved along swiftly as he compensated for the loss of a limb.

One day a roommate's boss approached him and asked if he wanted to drive cars to the auto auction after they've been repossessed. So being open for *just about anything,* he began driving long hours at all times of the day and night to many different counties in southern California behind the wheel of many different makes and models of cars and trucks (some had stick shifts). It was only a week or so until Mr. J. asked him if he wanted to learn the repo business. That's all it took!

It was May 1985, and from that point on, Lefty had found his warrior roots in his Indian heritage of the twentieth century as an auto repossessor! It was the getting used to *not sleeping* that was the most difficult and *very dangerous.*

That was one of the main reasons he got out the business. Five hours of sleep broken in two parts in a twenty-four-hour period was not only relentless, but the migraine headaches were crippling, to say the least.

In fact, that was when his sobriety date started. Once he got off narcotic pain pills, his spiritual life excelled.

Lefty has been keeping a journal since 1976 (it was suggested by his first sponsor in the program). So fortunately, a lot of *One-Armed Bandit* has been *archived in full detail.* All he had to do was *just* relive each crazy event on paper so you, the reader, can ride along "shotgun" through the streets of Los Angeles.

You can read more about Lefty from his website, *www.leftysway.com.*

The 300 Pound Lap Dance
Written and experienced by: Michael S. Forcier

When in situations such as the predicaments I find myself in *every night*, the folks I take from become very resourceful... *to say the least*. In the heat of the moment I have witnessed some of the most **bizarre** events when interacting with these "Desperados."

This is just *one* of *hundreds*.

What if **you** found yourself as one of *my victims*? Up to *what lengths* are you willing to go to keep from having your most prized possession *taken from you*?

You had just been woken up out of a dead sleep by a relentless car alarm. Glancing at the clock you realized that being only 4 AM; this may not be just an accidental occurrence. Besides that annoying siren is...

Your car alarm!

Jumping to your feet, you didn't give the blood time to flow to your head, so with your equilibrium off a bit, you fell back into the bed. Rolling onto your feet you fumbled putting on your slippers, or for that matter, *your robe*. Running down the steps and across the dark living room to the door is where the coffee table caught your attention... and your shin bone. *"Ahhh! God damn it!"*

The sharp pain was blocked out by adrenalin, as you hobbled on one foot to the entryway. By the time you're able to open the front door, you witnessed the Nissan 300 ZX, that you were only two payments behind on, rolling out of the driveway and into the street. You were not only pissed off by this sight, but you're willing to go to any lengths to get them to at least stop!

Your presence was expected because of the alarm, so they should already have been scared. And with the surge of adrenalin that was pumping into your head, they had better be ready for you because you were upset, mad, and in pain! So, refraining from yelling, you hoofed it right on up to your car.

But what's this?

Here you expected to find a big, ugly, scary man, 250 pounds, bearded, and covered in tattoos, with a cigarette dangling from his mouth (just like on TV). What you were surprised to find instead, sitting in your driver's seat, was a much smaller, long-haired man with only *one arm!* He was pushing your beautiful car with his left foot, while he steered it into the street with his only hand.

The awkward sight caught you off guard and you were also surprised to find that normal instincts let you down as the thin man was not intimidated one bit, as he looked up to see you, a 300 pound black woman, dressed in only a slip, coming right at him with the rage of a Brahma Bull in your eyes! *"Git the hell outa ma car!"*

Your growl was enough to shake him out alone, but as you reached in to grab him by his light brown, naturally curly locks, he got your attention quickly but calmly, holding up the stump of what was left of his left arm! And without looking up, he said in a clear respectful tone of voice, "Sorry ma'am, the bank has had your car picked up."

Now wait a minute! That was way too calm and cool of a response. Didn't he know who he was dealing with? *"Uh-uh, oh-no, that ain't gonna happen!"* Your response was definite and you are gonna back it up!

Apologetically but assertively, he spoke again, softly attempting to defuse your anger, "You can take care of all this in the morning ma'am and pick up your personal property as well. The police are—"

"You get the f___ out of my car right now or ..." As the last words (accompanied with all the spit welling up in your mouth) came flying out, you stepped around the car door and before he could decide how you're going to pull him out of your precious ride, you *jumped onto his lap! "You ain't taken' this car! You... You freak!"*

Your choice of words appalled him. After all, who is the real freak here anyway? *"Ugh!"* The air in his lungs escaped and the car lowered six inches as you planted all of your enormous girth onto his small lap. His thighs were flattened underneath the unbelievable pressure.

But you were justified in your actions. How dare he!

Without any air in his lungs, there wasn't much he could do or say as he tried to squeeze out something... anything! The tremendous weight was so immense, he thought that now, along with only having one arm, he was going to be confined to a wheelchair and an oxygen tank for the rest of his life.

"So if you ain't gonna get out, I'm a commin' along." Your action was justified, as you got comfortable with the fact of crushing out a human life!

Quick thinking was required if you were going to be a repossesser, but there was no "choosing the right words" when you were watching your life pass before your eyes. Somehow he managed to squeeze out a plea, "M-Ma'am, I cunot...d-do anything...as-s l-long as you're...on...m-m...ee."

You were kind of taken by his continued courtesy, but still you insist on showing no mercy!

One-Armed Bandit

"P-Please...you're...c-c-rushing me!" He was about to collapse under all the pressure.

"Sure, that's just what you want. You ain't foolin me buster. Once I get up, you're just gonna take off...Arnt ya?" As you barked out, still showing no remorse, you take it a step further by grabbing onto the steering wheel for support and savagely grinding down onto his thin body!

Pleading for his life was something he hadn't had to lower himself to in quite some time. But he had no choice in the matter, so he had to give it a shot. There was no crying wolf for him, he could tell that this crazy bitch was psychotic and was about to turn him into a quadriplegic after she jerked off his only arm, removing his lifeless body from her car. "Oh...ma...G-God...p-please! Ma'am...I...c-c-can't...b-breathe! You're...K-KILLING...M-ME!"

"Nope, uh-uh. Not until you promise that you're not gonna take ma car." Your wicked way was serious, as you just relaxed all that weight onto the doomed man just waiting for him to *"Tap out."*

It was time he reviewed his options: does he go the rest of his life as a cripple? Or does his children tell that sad tale the rest of their lives, of how their courageous father was crushed to death while repossessing a $2500.00 car? Valuing what was left of his manhood, he had no choice but to let go of his ego and gave you back your stupid car. He had no choice in the matter whatsoever, as he had lost the feeling in his legs along with the intense pressure against his rib cage, making it difficult to understand as he squeezed out his surrender, "Okay...I...p-promise!"

"Promise what?" You wanted a guarantee. Glancing into the mirror at the red face, you wanted even further assurance that this was, in fact, a one-armed man's last dying wish!

Amazingly he was able to make another response *"T...to l...leave...with...out...y...your...car."*

You felt satisfied with his last rights. So you grabbed on to the upper edge of the door and pulled your 300 pounds up and off the crushed man. As the car rocked from the release of your enormous weight, you turned around to see how badly you could've actually hurt this poor guy.

As he slumped over onto the passenger seat, you could not help from feeling sympathetic for what you had done. The poor man just laid there lifeless, not moving or making a sound. You bit your lip and observed the guy just kind of sliding out of the car onto the ground.

It took about two minutes for the one armed guy to roll onto his side and as he looked up at you with that red face and teary brown eyes, he responded in all sincerity, "Thank you sooo much Ma'am. I'm terribly sorry for all the problems. Just give the bank a call in the morning and you guys can work something out."

What country was this guy from? He was so apologetic...but why not? He just escaped being crushed to death! He should be grateful, damn it! You watched as he slowly dragged his feet over to his tow truck parked next door, got in, and drove away. "That's what I'm talkin-bout." You congratulated yourself. Great! You were victorious.

You climbed in the Nissan, reached way under the seat, grabbed your spare key. But you are having trouble. The key will not insert into the ignition! What's this...There was something stuck in there.

Upon closer inspection, you noticed that there was a piece of metal jammed in the key-way! "That muthafuca!"

Your scream could've woken the dead.

What he did, as you were climbing off of him, was a very old repossessers trick. Once he knew he was going to be leaving without the car he just risked his life for, when he had that undetected second, he put the "ball back in his court" by breaking the key off into the ignition. In doing this, he gave himself a good chance of coming back later and finding the car still sitting, immobile, because *it could not be driven*.

—Lefty

"Balls-Out in San Pedro"
Written & experienced by: Michael S. Forcier

Oh, San Pedro...

    A town with a beautiful view of the Long Beach harbor and the MacArthur bridge. Once you get all the way down to the park off of Gaffy Boulevard, the elevated view lets you gaze off over the Pacific Ocean. It's just breathtaking. Not a very large town but it is peppered with a lot of old houses and buildings.

    As in a lot of these older cities in LA, there are a few areas for us repossessers that just are not safe, mostly due to the high unemployment rate. And with no jobs, comes a lot of folks on welfare. Now I've got nothing against people on welfare, as long as they don't take advantage of the system, but many of them do. One thing I don't understand is how in the hell can people finance a car if they're in the welfare office once a month for a check? I guess the stud who is paying the child support is also shacking up in the same household, bringing home his check from "Man Power" once a day.

    Whatever the case, in my experience anyway, I've known San Pedro to be full of "tweekers" (speed addicts). Without judgment, certain areas in that town have a real negative "vibe" to them. Every time my job brings me down there, I have either a confrontation or a problem of some kind.

    And this day was going to be a prime example of how being just a little bit too brave in the repo business can be "real" dangerous. This kind of bravery can easily fall into the classification of just plain stupid!

    It was October 1990, and even though it was fall, it didn't mean the temperature was milder. I am from Michigan and in October, I'll be wearing a warm jacket even on a sunny day such as this one, but not here in Southern California. I was running "Day Shots" in Wilmington, a mostly industrial city twenty-two miles south of LA just off the 110 freeway a bit. I didn't have much luck as I expected I wouldn't. Looking for an oil derek operator who is out in the Pacific Ocean months at a time is like finding a "needle in a hay stack."

After an hour of cruising through parking lot after parking lot near the docks, I buried that order in the back of my clipboard in the "update" section. I was now looking at a repossession order for what was going to turn out to be a very dangerous and expensive 1987 Suzuki Samurai. The RO (register owner) was a name I was familiar with, but couldn't figure out why. It was not until I drove the short fifteen minutes into San Pedro and turned left off of Gaffy Ave, onto 12th Street did I remember running this address before.

The reason it came to mind was that I remembered the rather large, old, colonial style house on a large fenced in corner lot with no trees. How vivid in detail was my memory. Driving down hundreds of different streets, in what was at that time, my fifth year "jacking" peoples' cars, it did help in having landmarks, such as a sign post, in finding my way around one of the largest cities in America.

A Suzuki Samurai (SS) is the import version of a Jeep Wrangler. But not even in the same "ball park" as far as quality! If you've ever just sat in one before without even turning the key over, you'd know just what I'm referring to. After I had to drive a Samurai to the auto auction one time, I developed a serious case of claustrophobia. They are very boxy and rigid to drive, and that's without even look at the "Rollover Rating." That is one of the reasons Suzuki quit making them. Just as soon as the government came out with a "Rollover Rating" to help consumers, it was taken off the market. This vehicle was off the chart! It only had to be traveling at about 30 mph, and turn sharply, before it would flip right over.

I have a piece of equipment on my truck which is used only in repossessions with extended bumpers. These, and my "Go Jacks," were a prerequisite before I would drive a tow truck for a repo company. They are called "Quick Pins." They are two two-inch thick, solid steel pins, about ten inches in length and half way down they have a plate welded on them so as to keep them from falling through the hole that is drilled into the bottom bar of my Tow Sling. They are designed so I can back up to a truck and, without exiting Cindy (yes, my truck has a name), I can go under the vehicle's bumper, lift the boom, and as the repo is being lifted off the ground, the Quick Pins catch behind the bumper. They're good as long as the bumper is not too close to the front fender. A very useful tool for 'nuts like me' who prefer to work alone.

Notice, I said these are used only with trucks. Truck bumpers mainly extend away from the body of the vehicle, making it safe to go up under and behind the bumper without touching (or damaging) the unit. This is a lot more difficult than it sounds, mostly because I cannot see the contact my sling is making on the vehicle I'm about to hookup to, in any repossession.

My skill as a tow truck driver is always a huge factor when it comes to "hookin and bookin." In a normal repossession with Cindy, after lowering the boom, I back up to my prey, put her into park, shut down the engine (to keep it as quiet as possible), get out, and throw the hooks around the rear axle (if the vehicle is front wheel drive, the A-Frame). Then I run around the truck and in the same manner hookup the other side. I then jump back in the driver's seat, fire her up, and as I'm lifting the boom with my thumb on the switch, I drop Cindy into drive and slowly pull the chain taught. Then I drive off, always expecting to be chased!

A Samurai is kind of a truck. It has a bumper that sticks out, so I can get around it with my quick pins.

After waiting for traffic to clear, I turned onto 7th Street and drove three of the four blocks to my address. That's when I spotted a light metallic green (not a color I would've chosen) SS parked in the street, halfway up the next block, right about where my address was. SS's are easy to spot and after spending so many "man hours" locating cars for five years, most are easy to identify from a distance.

As I approach an address in the daytime, it's very important not to be made (noticed) as I am passing by. This can instantly raise suspicion. Especially if I'm seen looking in their direction. As I approached, all I was mainly concerned with was that the last three of the plate matched what was on my repo order...and they did!

Just my luck, as the house came into view, what do I see sitting on the front porch, but the whole "Fam Damily." What was this, a family reunion or something?

As I passed, I was able to take a mental picture of what they looked like...Ma, Pa, Brother and the sister. All bunched together on the porch. Even from the quick glance I took, I could see "without judgment" they were not a real "classy looking group." I was able to make out the bib over-alls Pa had on and brother was sprawled out over three or four steps like he was hung over (or retarded).

As I passed, I kept the same speed, looking straight ahead, and just prayed I wasn't 'made' (found out). I mean come on... it's like the elephant in the living room! When folks see a tow truck with no markings passing down their street that they have never seen before, suspicion is sure to arise, especially when a number of people are behind on their car payments, repossessers are *not* very popular!

I just kept looking straight ahead, pushing all the negative thoughts out of my head. As I reached the end of the block, I took a left turn and pulled immediately over to the right. What I did next is what I call my "fake check." When I think I might have been "made" when checking an address, I play it off the best I can by "checking out" a different address, just incase "the folks" are watching me. Now I've got to be really careful not to enter too far onto another's property. Because that opens up a whole different can of worms when Jerome or Mr. Sanchez comes freaking out because I'm checking the VIN number on their Chevy Silverado.

But that wasn't necessary this time because either my cool stealth move paid off, or 'Ma and Pa Kettle' just didn't care if the SS was taken off their hands. Lots of scenarios went through my head as I contemplated my next move.

What move?

Any sane repossesser knows there is nothing else to do but drive on and then hope the unit is still there sitting in the street when he returns that night. But not me, my insane thinking had me convinced that these "porch people" could give a shit if I just came around that corner and took that gol-darn money pit off their hands! So that's just what I was going to do, except, just incase they weren't as cooperative as I hoped, I reached in and dug through my toolbox, looking for those two heavy rods known as Quick Pins. I leave them buried deep in my toolbox, so that when it's not locked up and I get an unexpected disgruntled passenger riding in the back (see: Cold and Scared), I don't have to worry as much when they're looking for a "weapon of mass destruction."

Once I located them, I was only able to bring one out at a time (due to the one hand thing). This was it, I envisioned my plan of attack as I always do just before I go for it! This way, what ever happens I can be somewhat prepared...right? How does "one prepare" for something as insane as stealing a car while the whole family watches in rage?

What was I thinking!

Were they going to just sit and "cheer me on" as I removed their only mode of transportation?

It didn't matter what they thought, or did, because I've got my Mighty Quick Pins! Besides, by the time the folks realize what I'm up to, I will be up and under the bumper and pulling away before they can reach the street.

Now that is the type of grandiose thinking that can get a brother killed! That was one of my lesser points: rational thinking.

I worked each pin into its perspective hole on the lower boom and clipped the "cotter-pin" through the tiny slot on the bottom of each. This way they couldn't be pulled out by all the force. It was 6:00 PM on a mild Southern California evening and here I go doing something that definitely required rethinking (at least an alternate plan anyway).

Nope...not me!

Once I've spotted a unit, I will do whatever it takes to get it on my hook. This can be lucrative, but also can be a very dangerous way to do business. I thought to myself just before I put Cindy and myself in harm's way, "Do I need to remove every obtainable object that can be used for a weapon...just in case?" So I grabbed all the two-by-fours and all the loose tools lying out in the open, and put them inside the cab "just in case."

This is it...time to be a hero! This is what I tell myself as my heart starts to pump all that adrenalin into my head. Starting to back Cindy up, I refused to let any form of reason slip in as I dropped her into reverse. My plan was to just come casually around the corner in reverse, so as to not draw too much attention, and as quickly as possible, get under that bumper with my Quick Pins.

One-Armed Bandit

I rounded the corner with the cord attached to the boom switch whipping in my hand like a Pony Express rider. As I turned the wheel back from rounding the corner, I turned around so that I was looking without mirrors, directly at my target. I'm only going to get one shot at this...and it's gotta be right! What I was mainly concerned with, was that no "heroes" jumped in between Cindy and the SS like on many other occasions (read: Yur Killin My Mutha).

As I closed in the short ten to twelve yards, I could see the whole family sit up and take notice at this nut driving backwards on a collision course with their truck. Now I've got my doors locked and windows up for protection, but I could make out some verbalization as I lowered my boom just enough, to not hit the pavement, "Hey, wot the hell ar ya doin?"

Paying no attention to the hillbilly yelling at me from the porch, I stayed focused on making very sure that my boom went under the bumper before I raised it back up. So I stepped on the gas a bit more as I lowered it again, just for insurance. "Scrunch!" Now I was under the bumper!

Just as "Jr." was up and opening the gate I still knew I had the advantage. So I flipped up the switch in my hand.

And as the boom rose up, I dropped Cindy the two clicks of the gear shift into drive, and started to vacate the premises.

Without the SS!

Damn it! The pins didn't make it in back of the bumper!

"*Git the hell out-a here!*" That was the yelling I expected...but the kicking of my truck was optional. Jr. was not yet in-between the vehicles. He was focusing his attention with his boot onto my left rear quarter panel!

So I instantly backed up again, lowering the boom, concentrating on getting it right this time, I lost track of Jr. for a split second...

BOOM! BOOM! BOOM! Came his fist on my driver's window. "What the fuck are you doing? Get away from our car!" The spit mixed with chewing tobacco was being sprayed all over the safety glass as he "gave his war cry."

I ignored him completely as I gave it another go. But that usually gets them a little more riled up when I insult them in their shining moment. And Jr. was no exception. Especially by some crazy guy who is trying to disgrace his family by blatantly stealing the family ride... *right in front of them.*

So how does Jr. prove he's a man and get my attention all at the same time?

Just as I was failing at my second and last attempt to get this piece of shit wrapped around my pins, I watched in horror as Jr. reached into the back of my truck and pulled out something I never thought of as a weapon...until now. Out comes my 6" by 8"-5' beam (I use this rather large beam to put on top of my chains after I'm hooked to a vehicles front end with a spoiler, before I lift the vehicles up, to keep from damaging it)!

Now was the time warranted for me to leave...without the vehicle!

Just as the decision popped into my head, I witnessed Jr. put all 200 pounds of his "corn-fed" weight into that very large plank as he threw it...right at my head! Instinctively I ducked, as the huge board came smashing through the back window!

Missing decapitation by mere inches, I tried to drive away. But no such luck…I was stuck to the back of the SS!

I began to panic, as Paul Bunyan was retrieving the "battering-ram" from the huge hole he had just made in my back window…trying to kill me! One of the pins was stuck under the SS! I had no other choice but to just "punch it" and take the bumper with me before this carney turned Cindy into a "demolition side show."

Just as Jr. pulled the huge board away from the truck, I hit the gas and felt the SS jerk free from the bumper. Whew! That was close!

I did the usual look-see in my mirror as I pulled away and watched Jr. do his "Neanderthal Victory Dance." As he held the five foot plank over his head, he did a couple of insane spins and threw it onto the sidewalk as his tribe watched with pride. I'm sure that now "Pa" was going to re-write his will and leave Jr. all twelve of the chicken coops out in Barstow, because today he proved himself worthy.

Feeling grateful to have avoided losing yet another piece of my body, I rounded the corner rather quickly and got far enough away from the scene so that Jr. didn't follow up with his testosterone rush and hunt me down. Two streets and three blocks away, I got the 911 operator on the phone. "Hello 911 what is your emergency?"

This was the solemn voice I've grown accustomed to hearing. "I am an auto repossesser and I've just been assaulted doing a repossession." I tried to stay calm, but my heart was pumping so fast it was hard to catch my breath as I talked.

She responded in a monotone, "Are you injured and in need of an ambulance?"

I took a quick look around at all the glass covering me and Cindy. "No, but I definitely need a patrol unit out here…ASAP!" As I jumped out of the truck, I ran to the corner to see the street sign and continued with my location. "I'm at the corner of 5th and Louis in San Pedro."

"Were there any weapons involved?" She asked more of her routine questions.

I paused for a second. "No. That is unless you call a five-foot beam a weapon." I kept myself calm with some light humor.

"Alright, a unit will be there shortly. Please stay at your location. Are you still in any danger and need me to stay on the line?" She could tell by my high pitched voice that my heart was pumping through my throat.

"No thanks I'll be fine." My voice broke like a twelve year old, as I responded without taking notice of being covered in broken glass. My next call was to "Q," my boss, and I gave him the 411. I already knew what to do next, but the adrenalin was wearing off and the reality of what just happened was sinking in.

One-Armed Bandit

I was really surprised when two LAPD patrol units came rolling up, after only a short five minute wait. It was obvious to them after they took one look at all the glass scattered around the truck's interior and the hole in my back window, that this was a serious situation. After the first officer stepped out of his cruiser, I went into my usual rundown of events. Handing him the repossession order I said, "I had the vehicle in the air, but for some reason, it wouldn't roll."

"So what did you do with the vehicle…Give it back? And the RO answered your random act of kindness by smashing out your window."

Great! One hundred cops on duty right now in LA and I got the one whose wife is sleeping with his commanding officer. I knew what type of officer I was dealing with by his sarcasm. "No sir."

I went into more detail quickly, before he had a chance to go into some kind of "stand-up" routine. "I used the "Quick Pins" you see here (pointing to the back of my boom) sticking out of my boom. This way once I'm up and around his bumper, all that's left to do is raise the boom and off I go. Without ever touching my door handle." I thought I would win them over a bit with some light sarcasm, so I continued. "But then "Bo Bo the Side Show Clown" came off the porch, reached right into the back of my truck, and like he put it there, grabbed onto my 6 by 8 tow board and threw all thirty pounds of it right at my head as I started to pull away."

"Did he ask you to stop from taking his car?" The officer knew his Repo Logistics so I was careful in answering because I needed these two of "LAPD's finest" to side with me.

"That's the weird thing about it… it was like he wanted to kill me more then he wanted me to drop that fine piece of automotive technology," I pointed at the description of the unit as the deputy held the repo order, hoping he would see the humor in repossessing a '87 Suzuki Samurai.

"Did anyone tell you to *not* pick up the vehicle before you raised it off the ground?" The cop was now "playing hardball" with me. Most every officer of the law knows that if the party getting their car repossessed tells you to stop before we can get hooked up, we are supposed to stop from taking the car…right? Like that ever happens!

So my response went something like, "No sir, all I heard was some strange grunting as Jr. lifted up the weapon." There, I was not only answering his question but putting the focus back on the assault.

"Okay give us a description off the assailant and we'll go pick him up. That is…if you want to press charges." He already knew the answer to the question as he turned, without even waiting for a response, and said to his partner, who was playing secretary taking dictation, "Get a description from him while I call this in."

He turned back toward me and asked, "So you were sitting in the driver's seat of your truck, when he threw a 6 by 8 plank at your head?"

"Yes sir." I didn't need to add any color to the incident to make it look anymore bleak.

As usual, I completely forgot about myself being an amputee when Deputy Johnson came back with another attempt at his comedic future, "As if losing a limb isn't enough, now you got to go lose your head over something like this."

I stood numb and dumb at his sad and tasteless humorous attempt as I listened to the other deputy call in the assault to the dispatch. I knew now that they were going to go and arrest Jr. Most likely for assault or *attempted murder!* The reason I had a good idea that he was headed for C.J. (LA County Jail) was the way the fool just picked up that beam and tossed it right at my head without any kind of hesitation. From all the interactions I've had with these types in the past, I could tell by his violent behavior that this character was either on parole, dodging warrants...or both.

(To be continued)

—Lefty

Crack-Head Surprise
Written and Experienced by: Michael S. Forcier

Being the tight-wad that I am, I found it cheaper to work alone repossessing cars instead of paying a driver to ride with me every day and night. So I developed my skills rather quickly by having an instinctual degree of bravery. This was necessary if I were to be lucrative in this line of work. Working alone has not only saved me lots of money, but I was able to completely remove all the frustration that came along with a whining driver. Not only was I in complete control over what "snap decisions" I had to make, but I wasn't at the mercy of another's mistakes.

I know this sounds kind of foolish when I'm in such risky situations as I find myself *almost every night,* but I walked that dark path day and night always *"with my angels by my side."* There is truth to the saying that there is strength in numbers though. Especially when the chances are far greater of me getting assaulted by an outraged customer when there is only just me, with only one arm and no back-up (or witnesses). Even though I continued to work alone for 75% of my twenty year career, there were many times when having another body next to me in the cab of my truck would've most likely avoided a great number of violent situations. Especially when my life was at stake...

And this is one of those situations.

There are many communities in the area known as South Central LA and almost every one of them has their reputation as a gang infested haven for many violent criminals. One of these towns is connected just North of Compton. It's the city known as Lynwood. Now I wasn't aware of any statistics as far as crime rate goes, but I guess at the time the Lynwood Sheriffs Department was responding to twice as many calls per square mile as any other city in the LA area.

You see I didn't listen to the news or even read the paper for that matter. You would think that I would want to stay informed on my work environment, but no. Knowing what's really going on around me when I'm out there in it every night only makes me fearful, and as I've said before there is no room for such a negative emotion in my nightly duties. All that does is create a lot of doubt. Just a split second of doubt in any decision could make a huge difference when it comes to doing what I have to do all night long! Don't get me wrong, I'm not any kind of super hero who is above the criminal element. Oh, hell no! I'm just a long haired guy dressed all in black who is coming to take your car; who just happens to be missing his left arm below the elbow. But most of the time I forget about this sad misfortune and I need you to remind me that I am actually handicapped!

It was around 2 AM on a December night and the Pacific Ocean had sent the fog all the way to South Central, about ten miles inland. The year was 1992, and *crack* is a big epidemic on the streets of every major city, just like it has been for more then eight years. Unfortunately, it will be the misfortune for many addicts and their loved ones for many years to come. The addiction to crack is much more severe and ruthless, in my opinion, than heroin and speed put together. The reason is that the cut that's used to help the cocaine "weigh out" more, when smoked, creates such a relentless need to have more that the smoker transforms into a scary monster. In this state, a smoker would pimp out his mother just as he is exhaling *"just to get another hit."* Unfortunately I have found myself at that end of that crack pipe, so I know the intensity of how the soul can be bargained for.

I was running an address in, where else, but Lynwood this night. The visibility was down to about twenty yards due to the fog, so I had to slow way down in order to not only look for addresses, but to ID any vehicles that matched the description of the '89 Ford Taurus that I was looking for.

The Taurus is one of those economical cars that Ford put out. They were affordable enough that the car dealers were rolling quite a few off their lots. What that means is since I didn't have a license plate to go by, and it wouldn't of mattered anyway because license plates can be changed, I would be "VINing" (checking the VIN number) every Taurus within a four block radius.

Fortunately this didn't have to happen…this time. Because not three houses down from the address did I spot a Silver Ford Taurus jammed in between a mini-truck and another sedan. If this Taurus wasn't deliberately wedged up against these two cars, the driver was going to be pretty pissed off, when he tried to pull out to go to work in the morning. I could tell though that this "jamming of the bumpers" was deliberate. But I have my ways to deal with just such a situation.

Now remember that when doing any type of repossession, it's very important not to leave any marks on the vehicles involved. Sometimes, this is almost impossible, but I do my best. Even though it was late at night and there wasn't much traffic, this little procedure was going to completely block the street for five or ten minutes, at least! So I had to be quick and careful! Fortunately the street was wide enough, so I had just enough room to pull the car out far enough before I would connect with one on the opposite side of the street.

So I put Cindy in such a position that she was completely vertical off the bumper of the Ford. I jumped out and took one "J" (tow) hook off the boom and, while reaching all the way across under the front of the car, I hooked it into the "A-Frame" of the passenger side. I crawled back out and placed the other hook around a piece of the frame, far enough behind the drivers side wheel that when the chain pulled, it wouldn't come in contact with the tire (in theory). Then, because the vehicles where up against one another, I took a special piece of fiberglass and wedged it between the bumpers, so they wouldn't scrape against each other. Next, I took out one of the four containers of water I keep handy (I have tools for every situation) and dumped it out in front of each wheel, so the car would slide easier.

As I got prepared for the big extraction, I quickly ran down my short list of what was needed to get this car out from this difficult situation in order to *hook and book*. Jumping back in behind the wheel and dropping her into drive, I pulled the chain taught by slowly inching forward. Once I felt the "Cindy Jerk" from the weight of the repo, I pushed down on the gas gunning the engine, and "just like butta" I watched through the back window as the Taurus squeezed out of the parking spot, leaving the other two cars filling up part of the hole left by their missing friend. It was definitely wedged in on purpose.

Cool, no alarms went off and there were no signs of damage by the jerking sensation as I pulled it out. Just as I stepped out onto the pavement to re-hook, I heard footsteps...fast footsteps. Someone was running! The weird thing was, because of the fog, I couldn't tell from what direction they were coming. But I was sure of one thing...

There was more then one!

My first thought was, this couldn't be the RO because they came from so far away; how could they have heard or even seen me? Just as I pulled myself back up onto the seat and out of harms way, the hurried footsteps came right up behind me. I don't know what I sensed first, the smell or the sight.

Before I could reach for the door, a very sweaty black man grabbed my arm and at the same time, thrust his other hand right up against my stomach. It wasn't until I reacted with anger instead of fear did I feel the sharp tip of a knife poking through my jacket as I yelled my war cry, *"Repossession!"*

Their response told me instantly that this wasn't at all what I thought it was. "F___ you white boy! Gimmy dat wallet!" At the same time the man angrily spat out the words, he was helping himself to the inside of my jacket pocket!

I wasn't going to just sit and take this, so as I pushed his hand out of my jacket, I spit right back at him, *"I don't have a fucken wallet!"*

Now, I'm not sure if it was bravery or stupidity by the way I was reacting, **but I liked it**! I pushed the hand yielding the knife out of the way "without showing assault" as the sweaty man, began rifling through all my pockets now with both hands, one after the other. I avoided his quick advances the best I could with only one hand, the whole time trying not to piss him off. It was like a game of mumbly-peg.

That's when I noticed out of the corner of my eye, a *gun being pointed at my head,* from the now very present, second man. This guy was in worse shape than "his partner in crime." He and the gun were shaking uncontrollably as he stuttered out his attempt for me to give up my booty, *"J-just give us y-your wallet a-asss 'ole!"*

I think it was the way that this goof was handling the gun, or if they were going to hurt me they would've done it already, but whatever I was feeling, I didn't take his threat seriously! By not acknowledging the fact I had a gun pointed at my head, I was able to avoid that negative surge of fear that naturally would happen in situations such as this.

My just ignoring him must have affected his "big gun slinger moment" so he sheepishly put the weapon back into his waist band as he just joined in on the ransacking of the truck cab. "Sweaty boy" #1 was now through with all five of my jacket pockets and began to get a little bit more personal by jamming his hand into my left front pants pocket!

"Get the hell outta there!" I jerked away as I snapped at the aggressive advance from the desperate man. In spite of the risk, I had to set up some kind of boundaries. Besides, who puts their wallet in their front pocket anyway!

I watched as both of these crazed men just threw things all about the cab as they looked for the wallet that was safely tucked away in my bag in one of the toolboxes in the bed of my truck. I knew it was just a matter of time before this situation was going to come to a dead end as the two would reach the same decision not to pursue their frantic search any longer. And that was the angry finish I was **not** looking forward to! Sweaty (former Gun Slinger) #2, now was resorting to more verbal tactics for me to come clean with the cash. The whole time Sweaty Man #1 was still relentlessly trying to humiliate me further by stuffing his hand deeper into my pants pocket grabbing onto *anything*! Fortunately for me, I was quick enough to jerk out of the way, protecting myself from a sure rupture, as I kept him from latching onto my "Family Jewels."

We were now three minutes into this frantic "Search and Seizure" and by now the frustration of these two desperados was evident, as Sweaty Man #2 yelled at "Mr. Pick-Pocket," *"This punk ain't got no cash."*

The man pulled his hand out of my front pocket, stepped back, pointed his crooked nicotine stained finger at my nose, looked me right in the eyes, and said, "This is it you ass! Give us your money, or we're gonna hurt you bad, white boy...arm or no arm!"

I don't know where I got this relentless fearlessness from, but it was all that anger in me from just being violated that had me look him right back into his bloodshot peepholes and I said slowly and assertively, "I do not carry a wallet or cash."

Frustrated, but not ready to pursue his threat *yet*, in anger, Sweaty Man #1 reached onto my dashboard and threw all my papers onto the ground, and with a hearty "*f___ you*" he turned and kicked the papers like leaves as he stomped away in disgust.

It wasn't that simple with the "gun slinger," he was going to make sure that I remember him. I began to tremble in fear as I was waiting for him to reach into his waist band and shoot me with that gun. Just like they say that your "life passes before your eyes" before you die, I could see in my mind's eye the shot going off with his angry face behind the smoking gun. That's what my mind was focusing on, when instead of squeezing off a round to my head, he snatched my spotlight off of the passenger floor, stepped back, and just as he yelled, he threw that three pound lamp as hard as he could! At my unsuspecting head! BOOM! "We better never see you around here again! White boy!"

All my senses were alerted as simultaneously I heard the sound, saw a flash of light, and felt a sharp jab to my skull as that big plastic light came in contact with the right side of my head. I felt the pain just above my ear as I watched the spotlight bounce off onto the floor. Lying in painful agony, but "playing possum" at the same time, I listened to the footsteps run off into the same direction they came.

Damn did that hurt!

I put my hand to the side of my head and instead of a bleeding gash, I found a huge bump growing by the second. The pounding in my head began as I sat up and looked around at what I had to pick up off the ground in order to flee the scene. My vision was a blur as I saw, along my clipboard and all my repo orders, every piece of paper in my truck now scattered all over the ground!

Fortunately there was no wind, so I shrugged off the pain from the head injury, got down on all fours, and painfully pulled it all together. Amidst the blurred vision and throbbing in my head, I just scooped up piles of papers the best way that only a one-arm man could do and threw them all onto the floor of the passenger side of my cab. As I came onto the assault weapon that was cracked along the side from making contact with my head, a shot of gratitude overwhelmed me as I smiled. I was lucky to still be alive!

Now it was really starting to hurt as I thought to myself, should I go to the police or the hospital?

After getting everything back in the truck, I was able to drive slowly to the nearest pay phone and dialed 911. The operator's voice was both welcoming and annoying at the same time, "911 Operator, what is your emergency?"

My voice cracked as I started to form the words in my mouth to describe the crazy event that just took place. "I have just been assaulted by two men."

She came right back. "Are you hurt? Do you need an ambulance?"

I slowly began to disclose more information as I re-lived each moment, "Yes, I'm hurt but I don't need an ambulance...I don't think."

"What is your location sir?" Her voice was like a recording.

I looked up at the street sign that was fortunately right there by the phone on the corner. "I'm now at the corner of Lynwood Boulevard and Cherry Avenue."

"You're where?" Her voice raised a couple decibels as she questioned me in disbelief. The operator continued, "That is the worst neighborhood you could ever be in! Get away from that location and call me from another phone close by and I'll send a unit your way." *And she hung up!*

I stood there in disbelief from what I had just heard. Instead of looking for another stupid phone, I drove the six to eight blocks to the Lynwood Sheriff's station to file a report. There wasn't much of a lesson here to be learned, except for the fact of me giving in to their demands and handing over my wallet with all my identification and credit cards. The $40 it contained was enough for the desperate men to get a couple of $20 rocks, which is equivalent to about four hits off that "devil's dick." And for any crack head, $4,000 worth of rocks wouldn't be enough! I know I took a big risk by calling their bluff, especially with both a gun and a knife threatening my life. But I would not be in this line of work if I was easily intimidated… now would I?

"Thank the angels"

—Lefty

Doggie Do-Rite

Written and Experienced by: Michael S. Forcier

I earned my stripes as a "Private in the Repo Army" by having to talk irate customers "down" after just being caught stealing their cars.

This night was just "another day at the office" for me. Sometimes fun, sometimes stressful, but always interesting. It was 4 AM and I was already looking at the Nissan Maxima I had on my Repo Order. Even though I had a key, I was soon to find out that the car was alarmed with an "ignition cut off," so the key alone was not going to get it started until I could bypass the security system. I knew by previous experience in order to bypass the ignition-kill, I had to hold a button down, hopefully located on the lower left side of the "kick panel," and turn the key over; *both at the same time.* Sounds rather difficult? Try doing it...*missing an arm!!*

The alarm went off just as I opened the door and jumped in! *PHWEEP! PHWEEP! PHWEEP!* The sound was both annoying and frightening. (They don't call it an alarm for nothing!) Because now half the neighborhood was awake!

So I quickly reached across my legs, popped open the hood, jumped out, and in one quick slice I used my mini "Lock Blade," silencing the siren. That was all, but the alarm echoed off into the night, bouncing down through the concrete garage walls.

To avoid an assault, I jumped back into the unit and locked the doors behind me. Something told me that this was not going to go off without a confrontation. You would be surprised how many times I've set off alarms, even in driveways right under bedroom windows and no one has come out! Having a key that works the ignition makes the whole extraction process much easier. In other words, from that point on it was pretty much an inside job.

Just as I expected, the enraged customer quickly appeared along with a very large German Shepherd leading the way.

I was damn glad not to be standing out there!

The unshaven, overweight, Hispanic man, dressed in a gray sweatshirt and pants, put his face right up to the window and tried to communicate to me the severity of the situation. "Git the f___ outa my car."

As his large dog tried to eat his way through the other side window, I placed the repo order up against the glass covering his ugly mug. It was senseless to try and communicate with this guy, so I just let him "read all about it." Now, with his dog waking up the other half of the community, I was sure we were not going to be alone for long. With my head holding the repo order against the window, I made the 911 call with my 2-way radio.

The customer did not like the way that I snubbed him from trying to be his friend. So as I had the 911 operator on the line, giving her my location, my new buddy calmly walked over to the passenger side of the car, slowly pulled out a key, and began to unlock the door!

Now I don't know about you, but just the thought of having another limb torn off by Kujo didn't sit well with me, not to mention the way this guy was planning to rearrange my face. I quickly sat the radio down on the seat, leaned over, and held the door lock down. My unhappy friend tried to turn "that small metal object" with his fat clumsy fingers, trying to unlock the door.

Things were getting a bit uncomfortable for me at this point because now I couldn't communicate with the 911 operator because my **only hand** was now busy acting as the gate keeper. At least I was able to give her my location, before Home Boy "pulled a rabbit out of his hat." I just hoped she could understand the urgency of my situation.

Then, just as I thought things could not get any worse, through the sounds of the ravaged beast barking excessively, came another voice, "What's up man?"

Just what I was afraid of had just begun to happen. A thin scraggly white guy in "week old jeans" and a t-shirt was looking at me sitting in this guy's car. I was now out numbered and in what was soon to be a hostile situation.

My buddy freely filled in his hero friend. "I just caught this guy taking my car."

There was no way I was going to let this explanation go with out *all* the pertinent information. So without letting go of the door lock on the passenger side, I lifted up my leg and barely touched the window crank with the tip of my shoe on the drivers window, just enough to leave a communication line open from me and the "farm hand." In my professional, but assertive, calm tone I gave the guy a short 411 on what was **really going on,** before he made his own attempt at a "purple heart." "This is a repossession sir; 911 has been called. So if you just happen to have any warrants, you might want to think twice about getting involved." This works 80% of the time because most of these night owls have warrants. Especially by the looks of our new friend, he wasn't just rousted out of his beauty sleep. I could tell that this "tweeker" was on the tail end of a two week run. His face was so sucked up it was like somebody just opened up the release valve on his body bag. But I could tell that his adrenaline was still pumping from just walking away from his eight hour session of "Grand Theft Auto."

Just as "Thin Man" reached for my door, the customer yelled, "Catch!" and threw him the key!

So with my "knee jerk reaction" I slipped my toe from the window crank to the door lock, holding it down as well! All I could think was Thank God it was a two-door! In the back of my head was the fear that the 911 operator just happened to have gotten her car repoed just last week. So the calvary was going to be just a little too late to identify the body…If they even came at all.

There I was, spread across the front seat of that Nissan Maxima like I was trying out for the carnival as the "Elastic Man." "Skeleton head" gave up after only a few attempts at turning the key over; after all this wasn't his fight. Besides, the warrants that were issued for him on his "Failure to Appear" just became a reality when the thought of him trying to get healthy on LA County Jail food after not eating for weeks was surely disheartening. So he threw the key back at Home Boy and just walked away with out a word. Strange, but I was thankful.

I reached over and rolled the window back up and not a moment too soon either, as my buddy ran around to the driver's side. I was surprised that the whole neighborhood wasn't joining in on the fun, as Kujo's barking was still shaking the glass. Not only was the thunderous bark intimidating, but the site of those huge fangs, along with all that doggie drool on the window, was making me just a bit uncomfortable.

Just as Home Boy grabbed the dog by jerking back on his collar, Kujo shut up. It was now **"time to negotiate."** The man's rage turned to a sullen calm, just like Dr. Jekyll and Mr. Hyde. The big guy in the gray sweats with the huge dog attached to the end of his arm leaned over, looked through the glass, and with a puppy dog look in his eyes started in with his plea. "Listen man, I know you're just doing your job, but this is my baby! I got a lot of dough tied up in this girl. How would you feel if some "freak of nature" was trying to break up your family?"

Did he *just say what I thought he said?* What kind of "Good Cop - Bad Cop" role model was he taking after? This guy just ensured that the bank was going get a list of reasons why they should never give him his car back after that insult!

But I still kept it professional. It would've been way too easy to turn this guy into a crazed axe murderer after what I was about to lash back at him. Besides, all that was between me and becoming a paraplegic was a sheet of tempered safety glass. I had to be careful though, Homey could decide that one simple window repair wouldn't be that much of an expense, just to have the satisfaction of letting his dog loose for a little…*play time!*

I took the opportunity to press the redial on the two-way, only to have to explain it all over again to a different 911 operator. Hey, it's common in LA, there are many on duty. Some nights this city is just one big "911 party." They always say the same response, "Are you injured? Do you need an ambulance? **Is there a gun?"**

Now I don't know what this goof is capable of, especially since he just lowered the playing field with that "freak" comment. So as I looked right at the guy through the glass and while staring into his eyes, I said to the operator, "Yes, there is a gun... and it's pointing at my head as we speak."

Puppy dog boy interrupts, "So what's it gonna be Mr. Repo Man?"

The operator responds as a part of procedure in these threatening situations, "Do not converse with the subject."

Why lie? So I told this fat fool the truth (oh, but is he in for a surprise), "Just waiten' for the police."

The less said the better. Besides, I was just following direction. I really didn't want to answer for my little white lie once the cops showed up with guns drawn and didn't find a weapon...except for the dog!

That's it! Dogs do not like uniforms or gun oil. "Listen sir, I just wanted to give you the opportunity to leave the scene before the officers arrive. I really don't think that Kujo and them are gonna hit it off so well." Just as I began to talk through the closed door, I was forced to yell as that rabid mutt jumped back onto the window, acting like "OJ just put her pups to sleep."

The guy barked out as well. "Why don't you vacate the premises punk and leave the car behind?"

I guess at that point *the negotiations had been closed*. It didn't matter anymore because the moment of truth was soon to reveal itself.

Just then Kujo did exactly as I predicted. His slobber trail went from the side of this poor saps scratched up Maxima toward the direction of the two unsuspecting officers who fashionably appeared onto the scene in full LAPD fashion *with guns drawn*. Witnessing the whole event "drive-in movie style," I was almost certain the first cop was going to shoot fido as the big dog lunged at him! Homey was close enough to save the dogs life by grabbing his short leash before he was to find himself back at the shelter, looking for a replacement puppy.

"Stand back! Keep your hands where we can see them! Shut that dog up!" Officer #1 yelled at the customer.

Of course Home Boy was going to use his first opportunity to plead his case. Bad move. He didn't know **that he had a gun**! "I—"...

"You shut the hell up!" The officer was pissed from this "big furry" surprise. "Get down on the ground! And if that dog gets loose, we will have no problem putting *it* down...way down."

I just sat in the car like "a good little repossesser" and watched as this fool got the first class riot act.

"Shut that dog up or I'll shut it up!"

I knew that having this pup on the scene when they got here was not going to go well for Home Boy. And now he was going to be "tried" for assault with a deadly weapon...*the dog*. He no longer needed the fictitious gun.

Officer #2 came over and just like a valet opened my door for me. I gave it to them short and to the point, just the way they like it. Besides I didn't come for trouble. *I just came for the Nissan.* "As soon as I obtained possession of the vehicle, the RO appeared with a gun. Once he knew that I was a repossesser, he took the gun back into the house and came back with a key to get me out, along with a little help from that obnoxious dog."

As if right on cue, Kujo chimes in. *"Arf, arf, arf!"*

"Shut that damn dog up!" The officer was about "fed-up" with the dog but turned back at me and continued. "Okay sir we're going to get this all sorted out. Let me see the Repo order. If your paperwork is in order and because you seemed to have maintained possession of the vehicle, we'll let you be on your way. That is, if you don't want to press charges."

Was I dreaming? Was this cop really giving me the royal treatment or was I imagining it? Every time Kujo's dad tried to say anything, Officer #1 just shut him up.

After Officer #2 went back to his patrol car, I stepped out of the Nissan. While trying to ignore the crooked ice cold glare coming from the man who was *face down on the hard concrete* twelve feet away, I ducked down under the dashboard and prepared to start up the repo by by-passing the "ignition kill." After locating the tiny red button against the "kick panel," I rolled up my left sleeve and pushed against it with my "naked stump" so I could feel it depress. At the same time, I turned the ignition key and heard the engine crank over, starting up. The moment presented itself as "the coolest cop in the world" walked up to me and, while handing me back the repo order, says softly, "How do you do this crazy job by yourself? And on top of it all, you're missing an arm. I hope we run into each other again, that way I'll know that you're surviving out here. Be careful." He walked toward his partner, who was on his cell phone, standing over Home Boy who was unfortunately still *face down on the concrete*.

I made sure not to make eye contact with the man.

As if things couldn't be any worse for the guy, as I drove his car off of his property and into the morning light. *I really do like dogs.*

Thank the angels…

—Lefty

G-Ma and the Gangstas
Written and Experienced by: Michael S. Forcier

The first time I tried to repo this '89 Fleetwood from the area of 35th and Figueroa was at 4 AM on a Tuesday night. It was September 1992, and I was working alone (and will continue to do so unless specified differently). I spotted this older "boat" in back of a huge old house that was made into separate apartments. There was loud rap music playing off in the distance away from the location of my unit, so I didn't think that those playing it had anything to do with the "caddy" I was after.

I pulled around into the alley and into the cemented back yard that had fortunately a lot of maneuvering room for me. And it was well needed, because the front wheels were cocked all the way to the side, making it very difficult to be towed. This is one of the many tricks customers use to keep their car from being repossessed. Being a rear wheel drive vehicle, I had to "hook up" way off to the side of the bumper toward the direction of the cocked wheels, as to make up the difference in the direction of the towed vehicle. So while the vehicle is being towed, the front end will not hang out too far to one side, resulting in "what the officer who pulls me over" refers to, as *"Tracking"* or *"Dog Running."* Seeing how the Caddy would have to fit down the alley sideways once I got it on the hook, the normal thing to do would be to come back at a different time when the wheels are straight...right?

But not me! My motto is: "If it's there, I'm a-gettin' it."

It wasn't until I backed up to what I thought was the rear corner of the caddy did I notice how very, very dark it was back there. The moon was in its first quarter and no lights were anywhere to be seen. So I put the truck in park and crawled underneath the unit to wrap the "tow hooks" around the axial.

That's when I heard that "oh-so" unfortunate sound of my engine turning off! Then it was followed by footsteps walking away and up a flight of stairs. As I looked to the side from under the car, I noticed feet...*a bunch of them!*

Now was the time to break the silence and introduce myself in the usual fashion, "How ya doin?" I kept a jovial tone, without sounding like a smart ass of course. Most folks are never ready to be humored when they're getting violated in such a way as this. "I'm with the bank and they sent me to pick up the car."

I let my reason for being caught in such an awkward situation just hang in the air for a moment until in a grave "South Central" drawl, out came, "You'se in da the wrong hood... white boy."

A broken, squeaky voice continued, "Na ah! We don made dat payment. Ya'll better un-hook ar caa and get the f___ outa-here...now!"

I responded calmly, but assertively. Remember, one of the key points to being a successful repossesser is your communication skills. Always maintain control, no matter what the situation! As soon as I lose the offensive, it's over! But this is one of those bad situations where I was obviously outnumbered. And these folks can go from "Zero" to "lynchen-up the repo man" in less then thirty seconds! So there was no room for negotiation. I just had to get out of there ASAP! I thought the "simple mix-up excuse" would alleviate some of the tension. "Ok, there must have been some kind of mix up. So I would be on my way *but* someone took off with my keys."

"Can't do nuthin bout that, you shoudn been here in da first place! Jus put da caa down...now!" The "brother" responded excitedly, as the anger affected his "crack weakened" voice.

"I would if I could, but the boom works on hydraulics and I need the keys to operate it." I told it like it was. So with out another word, I "swallowed all that crow" and as I crawled out from underneath their over-sized chariot, locked up my truck, and left the brothers just standing there, I set out in search of my "keys to freedom." All I could do was follow the footsteps that went toward the direction of the music.

Right on up to the back of the rather large, old LA Victorian house did I *walk with a purpose* up a long flight of creaky wooden steps. This type of large house, that's made into a quadruplex here in South Central LA, could house three families, all in one apartment. Unfortunately in this case, this particular apartment just happened to be being used as a *"Crack Den."* Oh lucky me!

I reached the top of the stairs and knocked loudly and assertively on the door, anticipating the worst, like maybe a Shotgun barrel in my face! But after a few more feeble attempts of pounding, still nobody would answer the door. So instead of getting impatient (and possibly beaten up), I knocked again.

That's when a "Sista" (not of the religious variety) *cracked* it open (no pun intended). Without a word, she looked at me with a real guilty, confused expression.

I politely asked, "Where are my keys?"

She slammed the door in my face.

I was diligent in getting some kind of response, so I tapped the door hard with the side of my boot this time, shaking the whole wall. The same girl opens it and in a real "snotty" tone says, "What keys? Asshole."

So I began to put my boot in the door crack, nice and slowly, as I explained my situation. That's when she attempted to shove the door closed! But it was too late; my foot was in the door. So I had to talk fast to keep the tension at a low ebb. As I carefully pushed the door to "open up the communication line" I said, "No wait! You don't understand. All I want are my truck keys!"

Just as the words left my lips did I realized what I just subjected myself to: A dimly lit room with five or six people huddled around another, while he was putting a *torch to a glass pipe*!

Shocked to shit, I kept my cool and tried to not react to what I was seeing. I had to do this quickly, without incident. I also didn't want to have to keep repeating myself and get these fine folks upset now, do I? Besides they should be grateful that I didn't want a "hit". So I spoke loud and slow. This way I wasn't posting any blame and avoided any angry response. "Hi, I'm the tow truck driver downstairs and someone seems to have brought my keys up here by mistake. I need them so I can disconnect from the Caddy."

I felt like "Mr. Rogers" as I heard the tone of my own voice! It was as if I was "speaking in tounges" as I got no response at all. I felt invisible. Everyone was so high they were like "Zombies on Quaaludes." So I walked over to the stereo (what balls I had) and after *flipping down the rap music*, I said loudly and assertively, "Will the person with my keys please place them on the counter? I'll be right outside." And then I turned the music back up.

I walked back across the living room and before I stepped out the door, I realized what I was dealing with so I knew I had to get a bit more creative. Just as I thought, nothing happened. It was now time for "Plan B." I was desperate, so I walked back inside and started asking people face to face (but in a nice way)! "Excuse me, have you seen my truck keys, they are…"

It was such a wasted effort that I had to control my laughter in knowing how stupid my actions were. It was like I was looking right into the face of death as I tried to plead with lifeless bodies. I was in a third world country! No one would answer me until an angry woman burst out from the other side of the room. "I don't know what you're talken' bout white boy! And get the fuck out of my house. What the hell are you doin in here anyway? You got a death wish or somthin'? Give this punk ass his keys so he can vacate the premises."

Just as her angry words resonated through the music as if they belonged on the recording, my keys came flying from across the room and hit me upside the head! "*Boom…Kaching!*" It was sharp and painful as they bounced off the counter onto the floor, but I was relieved. I never thought I was going to get out of that HOLE! But now I had to deal with the brothers downstairs (and the growing welt on the side of my skull). Once I got back down to my truck all the "mob in black" did was try to intimidate me more by threatening me with my life...that's all! I tried not to make any eye contact with the four or five rather large hooded black men as I side stepped my way into the cab of the truck. Without shutting the door, I started up the engine as the obvious spokesmen for the happy group blocked my path from unhooking their ride.

That's when he got right in my face and with the *breath of death* he growled out, "If I eva see you-n dis hood-gin...yul be missin more den-n arm...Bitch!"

I still didn't make eye contact as I bravely ducked under his arm and, while I gave him my "empty promise" of not seeing me back there again, I quickly unhooked the car, jumped back in, and with a throbbing pain in my head Cindy and I pulled away as the mob waved with fists in the air.

But this wasn't over yet! Two days later in the afternoon, I was with my driver Russell and we just happened to be in the area of the 3500 block of Figueroa, so I thought we'd have a "look-see" and see if the Caddy was "accessible."

Sure enough, there it was unblocked! At 1:00 in the afternoon, tail out and wheels straight. Fortunately for me Russell was as "ballsy" and just as crazy as me. Most drivers are "chicken-shit" whiners. So I told Russell, as we drove into the ally, that there *might be* a confrontation. And if there was, to go straight to the nearest pay phone and call 911!

Just as I did on the previous occasion, I backed right up to the rear of the rather large, dirty brown car. With out a word the two of us got out at the same time and, after pulling the hooks off the bed of the truck, we had possession of the Fleetwood!

But, just as we got both hooks on...*Here comes the welcoming committee*! This time they were calling all the neighbors out for *"The lynching."*

Four of the committee stepped in front of my truck, while one pulled me out of the driver's seat. While dragging me by my dangling shirt sleeve to the front of the house, he snarled, "G-ma wants to talk to you."

While Russell watched in horror, the brother stood me up into the middle of about ten scary looking gang members while "G-ma" made her entrance. Down the porch, I heard slow steps with a cane, "Clip, clop, clip, clomp," as one skinny little old lady of African American descent, all hooded and dressed in black, made her appearance to join in on the lynching of the one arm guy! As the huddle opened up for her, she looked down at the ground while she dragged her frail body right on up to me!

Just as she looked up at me, *I freaked!* I was sure I was looking right into the face of **the crypt keeper**. That's when I was even more shocked when she wrapped her wiry cold hands around my throat and, as amazingly as it sounds, *lifted me off the ground!* She started to scream like a Banshee (with that death breath), "I'm tired of all you white folks pickin' on all us black folks. Why don't you leave us alone?"

While she was giving her "Inaugural Speech" (at my life's expense) my second thought was to pull out the 400,000 watt tazer gun I just happened to have at my side and paralyze G-ma! But my third thought over-ruled that option. As I gasped for air, I squeezed out the orders to Russell, "O-okay, g-go tell the boss that w-we c-can't get the car" (Oh yeah, and the first thought was that I was gonna die).

So I laid there in this front yard gasping for air while Russell calmly walked off to use the nearest pay phone. But not without one of the brothers confronting him as he reached the sidewalk. "Just where do ya'll think you're off to?" His deep voice wasn't that intimidating but the way he grabbed all 130 pounds of Russell and jerking him back by his sweatshirt really got his attention.

Five, count them, just five minutes ticked by when two unmarked cars and two patrol cars, zoomed up onto the front yard. Hooray for the calvary! The first out of his car was a plain clothed detective. Half of the mob had already run off as they pulled up onto the scene and by the time he had begun to exit his car only ten or twelve were left. You can tell that these cops really knew how to handle crowd control by their first opening statement, "Okay, let's see some ID's!" It was classic, as soon as detective Ramirez "popped the question" did Russell and I watch as, one by one, all but five of the twenty or so enraged lynch mob was left.

A heavy set LAPD officer walked up to me and, as he took the repo order out of my hand, looked at me through his signature mirrored tear drop sunglasses and in a low tone said, "You know that this is not the best area for you boys to be playing in." He looked down at the clipboard holding the order and continued. "Just three nights ago, right where your partner's standing, we found shell casings after one of these fine members of society unloaded a whole clip at one of our units. So if they've got enough stupid sense to shoot at us, how safe do you feel coming around here and *jacking their ride?*"

I knew he was trying to help me, but I already knew the threat level was high. So I answered out of respect, but had to try and curb the sarcasm, "Wow that's crazy, a whole clip."

Ten minutes rolled by and after they got everyone's side of the story and checked out my paperwork, they let us take the car. After all, we had full possession of it once it was on my hook and up in the air! And California law states that we are authorized to go onto private property to recover the financial institution's collateral, no matter where that may be. But there are a few exceptions, like government property and a few others (see: LAUSD Stand-off)

But wait...this isn't over yet.

—Lefty

To be continued

"We're Gonna Die"

Written and experienced by: Michael S. Forcier

Once in a while, when the opportunity presented itself, I would bring along a friend or an acquaintance, either because they wanted to feel what a real adrenalin high was like or I would pay them to "use their extra pair of hands" to help drive cars off the streets or to the auction.

Most of the repossessers use a "driver" every night as a lookout or for assistance. There is a lot of physical work to be done. Like for instance, once a night I have to get a car up on *"Go Jaks"* and push them around. But I can pretty much get it all **hand**led by myself. I always forget that everybody else does everything with two hands. And when it comes to the heavy stuff, I use my foot to help in the lifting. I don't consider from an outside observation how difficult it must seem to others as to how I do what I do.

I remember a Go-Jak incident when I began to get chased by an angry Samoan in his "tidy-whities" just as I was just getting ready to pull his car slowly out of his apartment garage. Once I got the front wheels of his truck up on the Go-Jaks, he came out of his apartment in a flaming rage. Not wanting to get to know the guy on a personal basis, it was insane how I took the chance of just continuing on down the street as his Chevy Blazer was **skating freely from side to side**, just missing parked cars by mere inches!

After that hair raising experience, I decided to drill holes through both the wheel plate and the bearing disk on the two front wheels on each Jak. That way I could stick a stationary pin through them both, keeping the dollies from "free wheeling" anymore. I should've patented that idea it worked so well.

Anyway, I'm not one of those repossessers who needs a driver. Most of them are whiney little bitches who make me feel more nervous than safe. Besides, believe it or not, all their fear feeds into the air and can cause countless confrontations. On occasion, I've taken with me neighbors, girlfriends, my son Michael, photographers (see: Picture the Butt Hugger), and I've had a couple guys from my old band Rager (pronounced: rajer) roll with me from time to time.

This particular morning I had a guitar player with me. Let's call him Chuck. That's not his name, but to save him all the embarrassment, it's the tag were going to stick on him in this crazy incident. In fact, this is the guy who introduced me to my third wife. I remember she told me later that when he brought her over to band practice for the first time, his instructions to her were, "Do not even look at the drummer."

That's all it took.

Chuck definitely did not have the balls it takes to be a repossessor, not even close! If you could picture yourself in some of these confrontations, when your life is on the line (sometimes nightly), you kind of get the idea of why every guy thinks of this as one of the utmost macho jobs of all time.

It was 1992, and I was driving my first very own Tow Truck. She didn't have a personal name yet, unless you call UAV a name. Yes, this was the ultimate urban assault vehicle! Having my own Tow Truck allowed me to freelance. This way I could work for more than one used car lot or repo company. But if you didn't pick anything up for them, they will drop you. With this particular car lot, I just happened to be doing so well that they financed the truck I was driving at the time. I would just keep transferring the "tow package" from truck to truck after I would run them into the ground after a couple years.

This story is a situation that occurred while I was repoing a car for "one of those" car lots. They're defunct now, so I'm allowed to use their real name, "Cars-R-Us."

Their "claim to fame" was that they promised to finance anyone! And yes they did. Here's how it would work: Let's say you just happen to walk onto their lot on a Friday night, just after getting paid, your pocket is full of $100 bills. Now, if you have ever walked onto a used car lot with no intention of buying a car, you better just keep on going straight to Taco Bell where you were headed in the first place. These salesmen are real conartists. Not only can they sell ice to Eskimos, but they're known to convince you "to beyond the shadow of a doubt" that your life is not going to continue until you drive off in that shiny red, '87 Ford T-Bird! All it takes is for you to hand over that hard earned "milk money" and sign over your first male child....in blood. Not once, but in eight signatures! So by the time the keys hit your sweaty palms, all you had to do, after you drove off their property, was fart into the wind, and that T-Bird was out for repo and back on their lot.

That is one of the main reasons I did not like picking up cars for used car lots. Not only was I getting previously run accounts, but the delinquent customers take shifts, watching out the front window of their home for the repo man. Not good! You never know what damage the previous repossessor caused when he walked onto their property for the first time, anything could've happened! That's what we call in the repo biz as a "burned" account. It's the worst when you unknowingly come skipping up onto the scene only to find a disgruntled old man in his rocker on the front porch, with a shot-gun between his legs. I know because…I've really had it happen!

We ran by the address for the Mitsubishi Eclipse around 2 AM that morning. And in that neighborhood I don't park and walk up to the addresses. I don't even stop anywhere on Slauson, unless it's to run in to the 7-11. This was three blocks from where "Reginald Denny" was dragged out of his semi truck and beaten during the LA Riots.

It was after one of those nights of running eight or nine accounts just to see eight or nine cars blocked in, and I was feeling **just a bit** overly anxious. It ended up being about 7 AM, when my frustration led me to the 110 Freeway and Manchester. So I figured I would drive north one exit and take a "look-see" at the Eclipse and maybe, just maybe, it might be unblocked. Besides, it was backed in, all I had to do is just "Hook-n-Book."

Now, mind you, 7 AM is not the best time to be *jacking a brother's car*. Especially since it was time to take the whole neighborhood of kids off to school. But I was frustrated beyond belief and was well into a "give a shit" frame of mind. Not healthy! Especially from past experience. And definitely not in that neighborhood! But you know me, with no off switch!

We jumped on the 110 Harbor Freeway to go only one exit! In morning LA traffic? I was already not using two of the three brain cells I had left after running all night. You got to remember that I only sleep three hours before I roll out at night, and it was past my morning nap time cause I had "Chuck in the Truck." I guess I was being inconsiderate of poor Chuck when I looked over at his frightened face after I told him we were going to drive by the Mitsu to see if it was unblocked.

"So what if it is unblocked? You're not gonna "rip it" now.... *are you?*" The tension in his voice escalated as I just continued driving with out responding. "Dude, if somebody is out there you're gonna just keep driving past... aren't you?"

I calmed him down with a little reassurance. "Of course not, I don't have that much of a death wish." I could tell by his fidgeting and the grip he had on the seat that he was not comfortable with that response. Besides he was familiar with my amount of courage (and insanity) after "rolling with me" before.

We were about two blocks away from the address when Chuck yelled out, "Let me out here! I don't like this!"

I slapped him around with a little authority. "Dude, (you can tell were from So Cal) just chill, will you! I'm only doin a drive-by."

As we drove two houses from the address, I noticed that the blocking P/U truck was still there. Upon closer inspection I noticed that there were **no people around**. So without saying anything, I pulled into a neighbors driveway, got out, and grabbed my "Quick Pins" out of my tool box and stuffed them into the lower towing "Boom Bar."

Chuck started in. "What are you gonna do?"

I just kept his fear at bay by responding with, "Oh, the car is obviously a "Non-OP" (non operational) and I'm sure they're going to thank me for getting it out of their driveway."

Insulting his intelligence wasn't going to work for long because he knew that our unit was blocked in. "Dude, you're not going to do what I think you're going to do...are you?"

Here again I didn't want to go into a long explanation of what I was about to do. Besides it being *highly illegal*, we were in broad daylight in the middle of South Central LA. "It's okay, nobody is driving either unit and everybody is gone. Besides, you do want to make some money...don't you?" The lies just fell from my mouth as I dropped the truck into reverse and began backing onto an abnormally empty Slausen Boulevard.

Chuck's silence was comforting but at the same time awkward, as I could hear him start to sweat. He kept quiet as I carefully rolled up and under the bumper of the older model Ford Ranger. With the remote control in my hand, I was able to push the three way toggle switch up, while keeping my truck in reverse, so that the bumper of the Ranger would slide back onto the pins. As soon as I saw the rear wheels come off the ground I did a quick look around for any witnesses and, just as Chuck put in his expected warning, I pulled the truck away from blocking the Eclipse.

He was gripping the dash board as he chimed in, "I don't like this."

The front driveway of the four unit apartment building was all concrete, so I had no problem in finding a place to drop the Ford right next to my Repo. After dropping the truck, I pulled just past the curb, threw the UAV in park, jumped out, and jerked the "Quick Pins" out of the "Tow Boom," throwing them into the bed of my truck. I didn't expect Chuck to help in any way.

I climbed back in and "made my move" for the Mitsubishi. To keep him occupied, I gave Chuck his orders, "Let me know if anybody comes flying out of the apartment." I lowered the boom just a bit too far, trying to get under the low front end of the faded red car. *Grrrunch!* A loud grind was heard and we felt my truck stop dead as the skid-plate ground into his driveway. Chuck added the audio, "Oh shit!"

I dropped it into drive and lurched forward, while pulling the toggle up to un-earth the heavy Tow Boom from the customer's driveway. Back in reverse, I went under the front end of the Eclipse. In what seemed to be one quick swoop, I barked out to Chuck, "Hook up!"

I threw the truck back into park and jumped back out. In what seamed like one single move, I had my "J-Hook" off the truck bed, around the "A Frame," and was surprised to see that Chuck was right there with me as we both simultaneously slotted the tow chains into the lower boom slots.

That's when my luck began to run out.

Once back in the UAV, I watched in my right mirror for the front wheels of the Mitsu to come off the ground. In the corner of my eye, I saw the iron security door of the upstairs apartment come swinging open; slamming into the wall, shaking the whole building.

Even though I heard Chuck start in with is frantic cries, I knew that I had plenty of time to be out onto Slausen Boulevard before the six foot, 280 pound Afro-American was close enough to become a threat to my exiting off the property with his eighteen day delinquent repo. "Go! Go! Go!"

Chuck was closest to the enraged customer, as he shook the building by flopping down the two flights of stairs, willing to do God knows what to keep us from leaving with his ride. This is when my heart sank in my chest after I pushed onto the gas peddle expecting to be driving away.

Instead, the truck was held back from the front wheels *locking up* on the Eclipse! I thought for sure that it was out of gear! *Dugh*...maybe it wasn't front wheel drive after all!

Chuck slammed the lock down on the door and went into some kind of airplane crash position by putting his head down between his legs.

I had no choice but to punch down onto the accelerator and drag the car into the street. Normally I would've stopped there because I just proved I had full possession of the vehicle by getting it off of his property. But Chuck's panic attack was having its affect on me. I just *kept on going* dragging it on the wrong side of the street, past the two houses to the corner.

As I glanced up into my rearview mirror, I was surprised to see that the big man wasn't ready to expose himself to the world in his underwear and wasn't taking up the chase...*yet!* I found from past experience that just because a RO (registered owner) goes back into their home, it doesn't mean that there giving up... not even! So I continued dragging that poor car around the corner and all the way down the next block! As the tires screamed, I couldn't help to see the cloud of smoke coming from the car as the locked up tires dragged down the street! I just blocked that God awful noise out of my head as I savagely pulled the poor car *two more blocks*.

Whatever "Jamal" had planned, I knew by default that it couldn't be good! Sure enough, as if right on cue, Chucky boy starts in, "Oh my god, here they come!"

As I jumped out of the truck to re-hook, I noticed that down the street coming towards us, was what looked like two LA Raider full backs running at full speed to the goal line. It doesn't matter how much experience I've had in the past in this area, somebody was about to get hurt. And I wasn't up for a ride in an ambulance! I know that I could've probably "talked these guys down" if I was in the right frame of mind. But there was this neurotic, freaked out twenty-five year old boy screaming at the top of his lungs, acting like a twelve year old jumping up and down in the front seat of my truck. So I too *began to panic!*

As if the tape was being fast forwarded, I unhooked the car, jumped back in the truck, spun around, and re-hooked to the front end of the car. I would've won the gold medal if there was such an event in the Olympics. I rolled over the hood of the small car, getting the other chain secured. In a blur, I had that Eclipse re-hooked and up in the air as we were ready to make our escape, all in a matter of forty-five seconds (with no help from the "basket case" in the front seat)! Even though the angry mob was closing in, my only relief was in the knowing that the car would now roll freely "out of harm's way."

Normally once you drag a car on the wheels that the e-brake is locked onto, the weight of the car makes it so the brakes cannot hold. That is, unless the car is too light, in which unfortunately in this particular situation, was just what happened.

As certain death was fast approaching at less than one hundred feet away, I dropped the UAV into drive. As I pulled away, my gut tightened up further as the wheels did not turn at all! I was forced to *drag this car again* away from the scene and fast! I had to get out of there ASAP, until I could safely access the car and somehow remove the brake. That's when, among all that tension, did Chucky finally get into the mix by yelling out a warning, "Look out!"

Just as his cry rang out, I felt a sharp, blinding pain as my head fell to the side. As I instantly came to, I was looking at a twenty-five foot metal tape measure lying in my lap. From over thirty feet away, this guy pitched that tape measure right into the "strike zone:" up-side my head.

Damn! Did it hurt! As I felt the warm trickle of blood run down my neck, I shifted into full on survival mode. While I began to frantically screech away from the scene, dragging that poor car away at a faster than normal rate of speed, I saw that "the Brothers" had shifted gears as well.

But now they were running in the **opposite direction**. They saw the insanity they were up against as I went screeching around the corner. Obviously they were going to pick up the chase, but this time in another vehicle.

"Oh shit! Oh mother of God!" Chuck was already giving us our last rights.

"Shut the f___ up!" I did not need any more of his drama. I felt like knocking him unconscious. I was so pissed off and... *scared!* Not only was my head throbbing in pain with a "gun shot size" hole in my head, but I too was beginning to freak-out as well. But I definitely did not want Chucky Boy to sense that. I had to stay in control the best I could of a rapidly deteriorating situation. These characters looked desperate and I did not want to let those "Repo Fears" to start clouding my decisions

Sadly enough, I knew that *there was no place to hide*. The tracks that the dragging car was leaving were easy enough to follow that a three year old could find us! Damn this insidious dedication to my job. I would have settled for flipping burgers at this point. Why I didn't just jump out and leave this car unhooked in the alley is beyond me.

That's it... the alley!

So I turned into the first one I came to. It would be a bit more difficult for them to track me on dirt dragging the car (who was I kidding) as opposed to following the thick black tire tracks I was leaving behind on the asphalt. It's difficult to think rationally when you're in a panic. It wouldn't have mattered where I dragged this car to, they were going to find me!

Two dusty blocks into my new off road experience, I looked in my side mirror and saw the pickup truck I had moved previously. Appearing through the twenty foot cloud of dust was the green Ranger gaining on us with ease.

Just as if my nightmare couldn't get any worse, Chucky Boy found a new pitch in his now changing screams, "We're gonna die! We're gonna die!" His frantic cries were out of control as his hysteria could no longer be ignored. "He's got a gun—and he's gonna shoot us!"

I kept my tone calm as I did my best in responding to Chuck's plea for life. "This guy is certainly going to a lot of trouble to chase us down. Maybe he just wants something out of the car." I could only see one figure in the truck. Just as Jamal got within hearing distance (as we were grinding what was left of the wheel hubs into the dirt) I could hear him scream, "I just want my tools!"

Seeing how he was out numbered (aside from the crying and whimpering twenty-five year old), I decided he was not going to give up. So I took a chance and stopped. Besides, I had dragged this Mitsubishi for at least a mile. And not only was there no rubber left on the rear tires, but I had ground the complete wheel hubs *down to the axle!*

Of course, Chuck freaked out as the parade came to an end! "No!" As he screamed, he jumped out and went running down the alley to "God knows where."

I calmly placed a paper napkin that I pulled out of my seat up against my bleeding head. It was *finally* over! Whatever was going to happen now was in God's hands. I wouldn't have stopped if I thought that my life was in any more danger. I was willing to drag this car right on up to the local police station if I had to (see: G-Ma and the Gangstas II). I watched in my left mirror as the large man with no shirt and blue jeans rushed out of his car and right up to my window. I'm sure that my calm demeanor (not to mention that I had my stump hanging out the window covered in blood) and the non-threatening manner in the way I spoke to the angry man kept him from acting out violently.

"Hey brother, all I want are my tools. I don't care about this piece of shit, especially since there are no rear wheels!" He looked back at the now light "brown" car resting on its trunk, hanging helplessly off my hook.

Of course I cooperated. "Sure man, get your stuff and I can get the key from you after you're done."

Chuck watched from the shadows as the RO got his tools out and handed me over the keys without any further altercations. Then he drove off without another word, backing down the ally and disappeared in a cloud of dust.

I unhooked the now piece of junk that was no longer worth all the effort, drove around the block, and backed up the same ally to re-hook. Chuck began to apologize for his childish behavior, but I cut him off by telling him that I too was just as scared but hurt even worse! As I cringed from the pain, I put my hand against the bloody hole on the side of my head. I know you're probably thinking, "How I was going to explain the damage done to the repo to the client?" Well it's like this…When my life is being threatened, I can **paint a pretty good picture** for them.

—Lefty

Laying and Lying

Written and experienced by: Michael S. Forcier

Every once in a while I find myself in one of those situations when the RO (registered owner of the vehicle) tries to *call my bluff* during a repossession. Here you will find out, once again, just how resourceful they can get when their "rug is about to be jerked out from underneath them."

The city is El Monte and it is classified as somewhat East LA. It has all the makings of a normal major Hispanic city, east of Los Angeles. It was a mild summer afternoon around 75 degrees. The year was 1989, and I was well into my fourth year of my illustrious career. I was in my second truck, a 1987 Ford F250. It had all the equipment from the tow truck that was handed down to me from the guy who got me started in this business, "Mr. J." He had a lot of great equipment on this truck, such as a chrome Tow Boom that looked sharp! The solid steel toolboxes that were wrapped all around the bed of the truck were big enough to contain a small army of midgets, ready to jump out and defend me in a time of need. It also had an electric winch that was strong enough to drag a car out of a parking spot. But the coolest thing of all was a giant "Push Bumper" that was of 1/4 inch steel. It was so strong that I could slam into a wall going ten miles per hour without damaging it. It did end up being damaged after I wrapped it around a new Chevy Silverado when I totaled my truck nodding out in evening west bound traffic on the 10 Freeway at the Freemont exit just east of LA.

In fact I remember a time when I was out in the middle of nowhere San Bernardino County, in the middle of the night, and to keep myself awake I made up a game out of rolling down the country roads. Just as I came up on them, I would jerk my wheel off to the side really quick and see how far I could throw the mail boxes. It was destructive but entertaining.

I was hungry from only picking up one car the night before so I was hoping that the work addresses I was about to run would pan out. The account I was running was a "day shot" for a guy our skip tracer found. It was a possible job address at a small Mexican restaurant. She was usually 75% right-on with her locates, mostly because she knew all the tricks when it came to "gagging" people.

You would be surprised to find out how many people sell out their family members for an extra $100 of blood money... especially when it comes to the ex. Many times I would have to stop off at an ATM before I would get to a certain corner to pick up "the rat" so he could lead me to where the car was. Then, in order for me to not to get ripped off, I would give him half of the money before and the other half *after* I got the car on the hook (repossessed). I do this most of the time because once in a while I'm on the losing end of a scam, where both parties are in on it and I get set up. **Not fun**...at all!

This, fortunately, was one of the easier locates. When I got to the address, all I saw was a semi-deserted strip mall right off of the main street. Yep, this was it: **"Pepe's."** There were only a couple of vehicles parked in the small lot in front of the strip mall and neither of them was an *'87 Cadillac Fleetwood*. It's an unmistakable car, very classy and sleek, and with the color being champagne, it would be easy to spot...anywhere.

So I drove around to the back to where the workers would park. It was a dirty, burnt orange stuccoed building and the parking lot around back appeared to be in better shape then the front. Oddly enough there were more cars in the back than in front. As I came around the corner, I spotted two "Bob Tail" trucks with Pepe's name in faded letters on the side of the first truck. They were not parked next to each other, so I noticed a space between them. Noticing that space is when I got that all too familiar rush of possibility and a lot of the time I'm right on!

There it was, all shiny and tricked out, just as they all do, spending the car payment money on tires, rims, and a killer sound system. The stereo was loaded with so many watts, that if the 100 pounds of speakers in the trunk doesn't make the car jump, the $3,000 to $5,000 hydraulic system will. I always get a sick feeling in my stomach whenever I see a repo all customed out like that. The more tricked out, *the sicker I get*. Because you know that all the more money that's put into that car, means that it's all the harder they're going to fight for it, and believe you me, they will put up a fight!

I did my usual "drive by" without drawing any attention to myself by gawking at my prey. In fact I did just the opposite, by looking the other way as I passed, just in case "Cooky" was out having a cigarette.

Well I guess Cooky wasn't "anti-repo" educated yet because he parked his Fleetwood head in. In '87 most cars were rear wheel drive, making them an easy "Hook and Book." So I went around the corner to go over my "pre-repo" procedure.

Seeing how close in proximity the unit was to the back door of the restaurant, this situation definitely warranted a call to the El Monte P.D. There was a very good chance of this being a nasty confrontation. Yes, it is very important to have the cops on my side when *any* confrontation could happen. Just a few words with the local dispatch would be a huge advantage on my part. During that unfortunate moment when the disgruntled customer locks themselves in the car, after I already have it on the hook, it's a blessing in disguise (or uniform) when it's the "law man" that actually gets these desperate folks to "give-up the booty." Or like the time the guy locked both of his Doberman Pinchers in his GMC pick up thinking *that* was going to stop *me* from taking his car? We just left them in the vehicle until he picked the truck up from our lot. Then there was the goof who wrapped a logging chain around his rear axial and padlocked the other end *onto his garage door.* Well I'm sorry to say that when I'm hooking up in the middle of the night in pitch blackness, I don't take a tour of the customer's property before I leave. After I hook up to the front of a truck, all I do is reach up under next to the transmission, flip the linkage down a couple clicks, and I'm "outta-there." Except, in this case, I felt a huge jerk and looked in my mirror as I was *dragging his garage door into the street*!

As I passed the address here in lovely El Monte, I got a quick look at the front tire situation to see if they were straight. If they weren't, that could make the difference from a clean Hook and Book and having the customer bear down on me with a chrome 44 Mag! So I kept driving two blocks to the nearest phone booth.

At the time my memory was a lot sharper and I could remember a lot of the police and sheriffs department phone numbers. In fact, I can remember Inglewood Police Departments phone number to this day. I've taken a lot of cars out of that city. In fact somebody asked me the other day, "How many cars have you repossessed in your twenty years as an auto repossessor?"

Well let's see now...I picked up anywhere from three to five in a sixteen hour day (and sometimes none). That's approximately twenty a week. So I'm just going to say a safe 10,000 to 15,000 cars did I repossess in my twenty years; relentlessly taking away your wheels right out from under you!

Anyway "back at the ranch" I placed an insurance policy with the El Monte Police by just letting them know that I would be doing repossession at that address. Sometimes they ask, "Do you need police assistance?"

A repossession is a civil matter and by "color of authority," a police officer cannot get involved unless he sees that the law is being broken (us getting assaulted). One of the reasons cops do not care for us very much, though, is that we do most of our work in that "gray area" between against the law, and with it. I gotta tell ya, there is a fine, "legal line that we walk" as repossessors.

So I drove back to the area where the, hopefully, non-event would be taking place. I didn't want to wait too long for a better opportunity because many times before as I sat and waited for just the right moment, I watched quite a few of my potential victims just drive away, never to be seen again! You never know when you have been "made" (found out).

Most repossessers sit and wait for "just that right moment" to make their move. Not me! The longer you wait to do the deal, the more time fear has to set in. In no time at all, you're so "gut wrenched" by psyching yourself out with what could go wrong, by the time you finally make your move, it's the wrong time! Me? I use spontaneity as a tool. So whatever happens, I don't leave "anything to chance" by spoiling my reactions. So however I respond, it's usually original, witty, and *always dangerous,* avoiding violence at all cost.

The stage had been set and with no time to waste, I parked on the side of the building and exited the UAV. This truck wasn't personalized like my last truck, as of yet. But it was in a class of its own. This "do-er of destruction" was not just a repo truck but was a full fledged "Urban Assault Vehicle." I peeked around the corner to eyeball the situation. I saw no feet underneath the truck, any cigarette smoke, nor heard any voices. And yes, the wheels were straight.

The only item that was making me a little uneasy was if the back door of the restaurant was open or not. Of course there is that big metal, iron rod security door that most businesses have, but that is just a cage door. I'm not protected from their seeing, or even hearing, me taking that huge chunk of their life away from them. I was hoping that the inside solid wood door was closed. But there was little chance of that happening; kitchens are very hot and need constant ventilation. Some things I just had to deal with. I couldn't let a minor detail such as **them watching me take their car** affect me now...could I?

So after taking both of the tow hooks off of the boom and laying them onto the bed of the truck for easy access, I hopped back in my UAV and put myself in *"repo visionary mode."* This is where I picture myself with the car on my hook, driving away completely undetected. This is very important for me, because the flip side of this is *a million forms of fear!*

I pulled around the corner and began lowering the boom. I got in position directly behind the Caddy and slowly began to back the four feet up to the rear of the car. I had to make contact with the bumper with the utmost care. It's almost guaranteed that this *overloaded* Fleetwood was going to have a motion detector on the alarm, if not a paging device, a G.P.S. locator, a locking wheel system, and two armed South American body guards lying down on the back seat! "Sure as shit," just as I made contact with the bumper the alarm went off! *PHWEEP-PHWEEP-PHWEEP!*

Even though it was just one of those generic sounding sequencing sirens that I'm so used to hearing two or three times a night, it still was just a matter of seconds before I was approached...or shot! I'm sure that you can relate to this being the most stressful moments of my job.

After throwing the UAV into park, I instantly "poured myself" out of the cab and onto the ground. Like a "snake on speed" I slithered along the ground to the rear of the truck, staying as low as possible so he would not be able to find me the instant he came busting out of that door blinded by rage! I grabbed the first hook off of the bed and in one quick swoop I wrapped it around the rear axial and had the chain slotted back into the tow sling in a blink of an eye.

Here's the part that we all have been waiting for: the grand entrance of the crazed customer. The tall thin man came flying out of that iron caged door so fast that it swung open hard enough to punch a hole into the stucco wall! He was dressed as you would've expected a cook, in grease stained white pants, apron, and you guessed it, a "wife beater" tank top. I had just finished with the first of the two hooks, when I heard the boom of the door followed by the usual, all too familiar, "Get the hell away from my car!"

He was looking into the cab of the UAV as he ran right past me on the other side of the truck. I waited until he was in front until I threw my voice more to the left side so he would come toward that direction, "Over here." In doing this, I used those very important seconds to roll underneath the tow boom to the opposite side. I reached up and got the other hook off of the bed, but unfortunately that included that memorable moment of our first meeting! My location was given away further as I slid the second tow hook off the bed of the truck and as the sound of me clunking that second hook around the other side of his axial, I got some kind of ladle *thrown at me* from under the car.

"Repossession!" I yelled out as the rather large kitchen tool skidded past my head.

I heard him scuffle to the left and as he looked down at me from the other side of the Caddy, *our eyes met!* But he surprised me with the calmness in his tone of voice, "Why are you doing this?"

The plea was simple and deserved an answer. "The bank has had your car picked up." Nothing more, nothing less, that is all that I had to say!

But that was just an introduction. I guess the limited explanation was an insult to Cooky, because this is where his mind "clicked" into survival mode. Instead of coming down on the ground after me, he ran around to the other side were I had just began crawling to my feet. Him running to where I was told me two things: first, his adrenalin was pumping and second, a violent reaction was most certain to happen.

Instead of him jumping on my back for a friendly "piggy back" ride, I stayed just out of reach as I heard his frantic plea as he headed in my direction, "You, you get away from my car!"

Now I am not going to disrespect the poor guy by just ignoring him. As I braced my only hand onto the top of the tool box, I answered so fast it was like I was auctioning off the car. In a second, I spat out my motivational reply and this was definitely positive thinking in action, "Just get your things out of the car, sir, and you can pick it up later, after you've straightened it all out with the bank."

But this is a lot to say when you got a 6' 4" pissed off man *coming right at you*! And by his actions, he wasn't coming around that truck just to shake hands. As soon as he rounded that front corner of the UAV I was in phase three of "close contact repo mode."

Now most repossessors have an "Eagle Claw" or a "Stinger" on the back of their truck so they don't even have to get out of the cab. They just lower the boom, extend those big giant hooks around the tires, lift it up, and there is your hook and book! But not me... I had some kind of death wish by challenging myself in having to get out of the truck, in every repo, and create a personal relationship with *too many* customers.

Now in phase three, of this happy event I, believe it or not, had everything under control. Just as Cooky was about to grab me, I jumped up onto the bed of the truck and in two quick steps gingerly crossed over the toolboxes to the drivers side. Before he was able to reverse directions and come after me, I jumped onto the ground and bounced right into my driver's seat, closing and locking the door behind me. Whew!

The look in his eyes, as we faced each other between the glass…was priceless. Not only was he even more upset, but desperation was becoming more evident as he knew it was only a matter of seconds before he was to witness one of the most important things in his life being towed away by some "lame ass" *one-armed* repossessor.

This is usually when the pissed off, frustrated customer either pounds his fists onto the window or reaches into the back of the truck for something to smash the glass with (read: Balls Out in San Pedro). If they don't have the criminal background to react violently, a few of the customers who have that much adrenalin pumping either climb into their car if it's unlocked (read: Ma'am You're Going to Jail), or jump onto the back of my truck (See: Cold and Scared).

But not this crafty character. Nope, not Cooky! What this desperate individual did was like a baby, he got down on all fours and went into a very dark place. Instead of climbing onto my truck, breaking out my windows, jumping into or onto the car, he crawled underneath the repo! Yep, he was willing to give up his simple life for his dream in what I call Laying and Lying.

Yes, this has unfortunately happened a few too many times before, so I had terminology to refer to. I had a name for this type of desperate behavior. And I'm not too tolerant when it comes to sheer stupidity.

With the UAV in drive, I lifted up the Boom and I watched in my mirror, expecting to see Cooky running into the restaurant to call 911. Instead, I was shocked to see a grown man behave like that as he stayed under his new shelter! So it was me that picked up my radio and punched in the only phone call it could make: 911! Whatever he had planned, I wasn't going to be intimidated by a foolish move like that. And I let him know it! I didn't put the truck back into park. Nope, I didn't even roll down my window to plead and beg with this fool. Instead, like right out of a horror movie, **I inched the truck forward!** I let this nut case know that *I was taking his car!* So if he wanted to see his kids open up their gifts next Christmas, he better roll on out'a there.

That's when the screaming started. "Aaaahh! My back! You're crushing me…oh…oh my God!"

Apparently the back door to the restaurant was open as I heard, amidst all the horrific screams, "Call 911! Call 911!" Little do they know the calvary was already on its way.

I didn't want it to look like I was purposely trying to crush this man to death just to repo his car (I've got some morals) once the police arrived onto the scene. So the stand-off began. And since it was still just the two of us, I gave Cooky a short reality check as he laid there in apparent agony, willing to give up his life for a material possession. "You know sir, once the ambulance takes you off to the *morgue* to do an *autopsy*, your car will be in the repo lot being appraised for how much we can get for all those nice, expensive, custom features you added before we take it to the auction. But there is a much easier, softer way. Just pull yourself together and don't worry, nobody needs to know that you're laying underneath your car. Get a couple of your personal items out of your car and after a simple phone call to the bank, you will be back on the strip showing off to all the ladies."

There was a long pause as I waited for some kind of response from this confused individual. I'm sure he was running through all his options in his head. Especially now that I put that "all to familiar" picture back in his head of Maria and her sisters with their low cut tops, all stuffed into the Caddy on a Friday night. Also he had to think real quick before the cops showed up. I continued explaining his fate, "Sir, I don't know if you're aware of the repercussions of filing a false police report, not to mention the embarrassment you will feel once they find out that you are a big faker!"

"You mother fucker...aahh...you, you broke my back! You're going to jail...for attempted murder and when you get out, we are going to hunt you down and kill you and all of your family! Oh! Oh it hurts...aaahhhh!"

I sensed *"Oscar Buzz."* This guy was as serious as a heart attack as he saw Maria's whole family at the awards presentation, instead of her sister in the back seat. Whatever, because now I could hear the sirens in the distance.

I don't know what his help in the kitchen told the 911 operator because I could also hear the "chop chop chop" of an LAPD helicopter off in the distance...and that's not good! Now high ranking police officers had to get involved and, being an election year, a report would be filed on my attempted murder and blah blah blah.

My head started to mug me as I heard the chopper fly away from the area. I thought I might as well give it one more shot, and this time; *show a little respect.*

"Okay Mr. Rodriguez," I continued to yell out the side window. "This is going to be my last request for you to climb out from under that car and avoid all the embarrassment. Besides even if by some slim chance they do find out that you were hurt, the vehicle is up in the air on the back of my truck, so we still have full possession. So you can expect that you run a far chance of getting it back at all if you continue to *not* cooperate."

The Oscar attempt continued with the weakest attempt at a moan I've ever heard. I've heard better from the cheapest of pornos. "Ooooohh...ahhhhh...uhhhhhhh."

I could tell from that point this was going to go the distance. Once one of these customers put themselves in this type of ridiculous situation, they never back out. I mean, come on, they *have their image to protect!*

As I saw the flashing lights from the police cars approaching, I got out of the truck and put on the "Kid Gloves." And with a sweet soft effort of shortening the time it's going to take "once those police cars pull up" I nicely said (and I *never* plead with these fools), "Please sir, I'm looking out for you here. I really don't want your kids to have to see you in jail once you've lied to the police. So come on and climb on out of there. Crawl out here and I'll give you your car back." What a liar! It didn't matter what I used for a ploy because I was sure that response was still going to be the same.

"F___ *you prick!*" He barked out, just like on *The Exorcist*, but without the green slim.

First came the black and white patrol car, then the red ambulance, and of course, what else, but a fire truck. The whole parade came to an end right in this parking lot. Oh lucky me! As they pulled in, they saw me standing outside my truck looking down at the poor sap under his car. As the first officer exited his car, I kept the situation calm by meeting him at his car and handing him the repo order while shaking my head. Initiating the conversation I said, "I called ahead to let dispatch know what I was going to be doing here. I spoke with Mary, from your station." Usually the first question they ask me is if I notified the station ahead of time, so I thought I'd get them on my side as soon as possible before Cooky went into his "Award winning monologue." And now that I had him listening, I quickly explained the situation, "I had the unit up in the air when the RO came running out of the back door and jumped underneath." I knew all the key points to cover and the less said the better.

He took the repo order out of my hand and instructed me to, "Go have a seat over on the curb while we sort this all out."

I respectfully replied, "Yes sir." As I watched from the street, I could just imagine what kind of heart wrenching, sob story Mr. Rodriguez was laying down. It wouldn't have mattered anyway because I already gave my side of the story and I had possession of the unit!

I'm confident that Mr. Rodriguez was boring them to tears with so much useless information. And these are hard critics to appease. The only problem would be if there was a witness. Like the helper in the kitchen!

I watched as the two paramedics crouched down next to the Caddy and talked to the new SAG member about his life passing before his eyes while he was being crushed to death. After a few minutes, one of the paramedics walked away with the deputies and as they spoke, I watched the second paramedic coaxing Mr. Rodriguez out from under the car. Whew! That was a relief. I was preparing myself for them to call out the "Jaws of Life." That told me that Cooky hopefully wasn't going to go for that Oscar after all. But he was limping off with the help of the paramedic toward the ambulance (bless his heart).

I turned and looked as I heard the footsteps of the other paramedic approaching me. His voice was low and soft as he spoke, "Off the record, I really don't think that this guy is hurt at all. But we have to take him in for

X-rays. It's protocol. Now depending on those results, will be if we are going to be contacting you or not."

I stood up and watched as the two deputies climbed in and drove away from the scene without a word for me. They must've gotten another call. Cool! That meant with Cooky going off in the ambulance, the Caddy was mine!

I caught the rolling of the eyes as the second paramedic was closing the door of the ambulance on Cooky, as he clung to life! He just shook his head at us, as if to say, "Don't worry, this guy's faking it." But he did walk over to us, I guess to say goodbye to me. He reached out for my handshake and said, "I can't tell you how comforting it is to see someone with a handicap like yours out here doing a job like this. I have a lot of respect for that. Take it easy, and be careful out there."

I just stood there in awe. I always forget that…*I'm missing my arm*.

—Lefty

The School Bully

Written and Experienced By: Michael S. Forcier

I have sat on this stake-out twice before here in Monterey Park, but to no avail. It was two weeks prior, when I staked-out this Nissan Altima until 8 AM, just to see the RO (registered owner) open up his gate and drive off in a different car. Thus leaving the Nissan locked up behind the gate. Then on another occasion I actually was able to take up a chase, only to have the male driver pull into a government building's secured parking lot. And there, I could get into some serious trouble for trespassing into a restricted government area.

But not this time. Nope. I *always* have a plan! This time I was sure that this guy was *GOIN DOWN*. Most of the time my plans do work. Partly because they've been "tried and true" in previous, similar situations and the other is the way that I "lay out" the stake outs. So no matter what happens, I either get the car, the account closes, or the customer pays up. I would much rather get the satisfaction (and the money) of repossessing the unit.

Not very often when I'm handling an account, does it get "burned" and the car disappears, sometimes never to be seen again. If for some reason I could not repossess the unit (i.e. it's always blocked in or never leaves the garage) I knock on the door and ask them to, "Go to the bank and pay it current." If they do pay up, I would get a closing fee for provoking the customer to bring the account current. I worked for a guy (and I'm not going to mention any names here) who, when he knew that he could not repo the car, instead of just nicely knocking on the door around dinner time, he would drive up onto their front lawn at *4 AM*, turn on the flashing emergency lights, aim all four 50,000 candle power flood lights onto all the windows of the house, and on his loudspeaker, *"call the poor bastard out."* Talk about insensitive!

In this case, I knew that the car was being driven. What I normally do when I assume that a unit is not being driven, is mark a tire with chalk, just like the meter maids do, to see if it moves. In repossessing the car, as opposed to just getting a closing fee, not only does the extra $70 help, but 80% of time, these same customers default on their payments again and I have to be a lot more tactful in catching them "off guard" a second time (read: ATM Reach Around) because now they know "I'm a-comin."

In this particular situation, the address was conveniently located just three houses down from the local high school. This was good and bad for reasons I was soon to find out, through an unfortunate experience, whether it was in my favor...or not. A few times before when I was on a stake-out close to a school, did neighbors call out the local law enforcement agency on me. Probably because they thought a possible sex offender was seeking out his prey in front of their homes. Not only was this very embarrassing, but once the police arrived onto the scene, in the process of the cops running my record to see "what priors" I had for taking eight year old boys to the movies, do I find myself watching my stake-out drive off without me being able to pick up the chase. So whenever I start my stake-outs now, I call ahead to the local P.D. to let them know that I am at a certain cross street doing a stake-out for the bank.

I never give them the exact address for a couple of reasons. Once I gave the dispatch operator an exact address of a stake out. And after she asked me to repeat it, she shockingly said, "That's my house!" Around five or six times, I've actually had patrol cars show up onto the scene after I gave the dispatch operator the address. Then the deputies took it a step further by walking right on up to the door and burning the shit out of the account!

This time I was located at a high school and not a grade school or middle school, so I wasn't concerned so much about being mistaken as a predator or a drug dealer. Besides, I was in my tow truck. But I did call in my intention to the local P.D. ahead of time, especially for what I had planned!

Now, when I am in my tow truck and I don't have time to "hook and book," I need to figure out a location that I can park my truck so that "when the RO pulls out of his driveway" he doesn't make eye contact with my truck. Mostly due to the fact that possibly for the next hour, he is going to be seeing me in his rearview mirror from time to time on his way to work. But there was no seeing me at all here (I hope)! This stake out was going to be very different...to say the least! Different in a way that once I finally do make *my move* on this car, my truck is not going to be near either one of us. My plan was to *"car jack"* this guy!

So I had to leave "Cindy" (yes, we did have a very personal relationship, my truck and I) around two corners, about three blocks away. There was a lot of preparation needed for this "special event" because of the plan I had devised in order to *finally* get possession of this unit. No more wasted time!

You're probably wondering at this time, why was this car so special that I would go to so much trouble, consuming up all my time? Normally I'd have "Kicked It In" (knocked on the door to provoke payment) after the second attempt failed at repossessing it. But during this particular week, work was slow. And the Nissan was still "showing." So having learned from my past two attempts at this, I now had to go into final and desperate **"car jack mode."**

This, I do not like to do...at all! Mostly due to the fact of all the things that can go wrong when I actually do a **car jacking!** Like beatings, guns, knifes, and possible *limb removal!*

The time was 7:40 AM and the streets of this neighborhood were filled with students walking to school. Since the unit was located almost directly across the street from the local high school, I thought that I would use all the commotion to my advantage. From my previous attempts, I have watched from a distance as the driver of my vehicle would walk out of the residence around 7:50 AM and, after unlocking the car door, start up the engine of the Altima that I was after. Then he would step back out of the car and, after approaching the gate, would unlock the pad lock, hang it from the chain link fence, fling both sides open, and return to the car, pulling it into the street. Here, he would put the Altima in park and *leave the engine running* while walking the twenty feet or so back over to close the gate. Then he'd return to his car and drive off to his fun and exciting day at the office.

After reviewing this procedure over and over in my head, my feeble plan was simple, but very dangerous. After he left the engine running in the street and exited the car, I would *jump in* and drive off when he was closing the gate. Sounds simple...doesn't it?

So at 7:45 AM on a bright, mild Monday morning, I parked my truck the next street over, and after I dropped the tow boom onto the ground, this forty year old was off to school! Once I walked a block and rounded the first corner, I joined into a group of kids that, as weird as it sounds, looked pretty much just like me. Dressed in a black leather jacket and long hair, I blended right in with my "randomly chosen" new friends. I thought that all the "freaks" went later in the day to Continuation School.

I received a couple of strange looks, as I felt rejected by the fact that I was missing an arm. But that was only a minor thing. Besides, how did they know that this wasn't my first day at school after moving here from Minnesota? And oh was I filled with many different stories of how a guy could get his *arm ripped off* working as an "Extra Hand" on the farm.

It was only a couple of houses that I traveled with my new group of friends, when I realized that I would get to the location way too soon. So I found a reason to stop and *pretend* to tie my shoes. It was the only thing I could think of to stall for time, as I didn't see "Mr. Nissan" out of his house yet. It wasn't until I got down on one knee that I felt very frustrated as to how I was going to play this tying shoe thing off after I realized that I...Only had one hand! It was such an awkward moment that all I could do was just bust out laughing.

So I walked over to the curb and sat while I watched and waited for the gate to open. I wish I would've brought my homework, because I had a good five minutes before...I got that real "sick feeling in my stomach" as I finally heard the "ching-ching" of the chain lock being undone and the gate was being readied to be opened! The gate keeper had finally arrived.

Unfortunately by this time, the student foot traffic had been reduced to only a few. But those few seemed to be unconcerned when they heard the tardy bell ring. So I stood up and, without being too obvious, I fit myself right behind a guy and a girl who unknowingly were being involved into "aiding and abetting" in an attempted Felony Car Jacking.

My eyes were completely fixated on the customer as he began to open the first half of the gate as my "motley crue" approached. The dark skinned man with black wavy hair was dressed in his tan business suit, all "pressed to impress." Too bad it's going to be all wrinkled and smelly from the long bus ride needed to get him to the office after his car gets jacked! I know I was being a bit shrewd, but it was important to get myself "psyched-up" before I did such an *unholy act*.

It was like everything was happening in slow motion as the seconds ticked by with my new group of friends. We walked toward the Altima, waiting for the customer to leave it running in the street.

But what's this?

After the three of us closed-in, while passing the second house, I was shocked to see that instead of backing the Altima into the street, he only went as far as *the sidewalk*, before Mr. Nissan exited the car to close the gate.

Oh Shit! This was not what I had in mind...at all. Now he was only one car length away from the gate instead of three. It's going to be very difficult for me to jump in and "Jack that Car" with him just a few yards away! He would only be *just on the other side of the unit* when he began to pull that chain link gate back closed.

But you know me, I very seldom abort a plan once I get started. That could be why I worked on "temporary repo licenses" for so long; I was uncontrollable. I was like an "Adrenalin Junky" with a deadly habit! Besides, I've pulled this dastardly deed off before, *successfully* (see: ATM Reach Around). And in my "crazy repo mind" I was confidant that I could "pull this one off" as well.

The Altima had Hispanic morning "Musica" blaring and buzzing in the speakers from the high volume, as I'm sure he was getting himself "revved-up" to face his busy day. This was good, because I needed as many distractions as possible in helping me get into that car as *quickly* and as *quietly* as possible.

As I observed him from about twenty feet away, my line of view was not obstructed as he began walking the short distance toward the first of the two gates. The timing couldn't have been better! As I blended in with the students, we shuffled along in no hurry "whatsoever" to get into the home room that we all so hated. There weren't many choices as to when I had to "MAKE MY MOVE." If I were to pause for just one split second, I might as well just keep on walking. The timing had to be perfect! A moment too early and I'll run right into the guy, and possibly *get pounded!* A second too late and I will most certainly get pounded!

I figured that the best time to jump in was when his back was to me, while he was closing the gate furthest to the driver's side on the right. I was only eight feet away, as my posse closed in. The unsuspecting commuter had just closed the first gate on the left and began to take the four steps toward the other when I split off from my new found friends by ducking behind the unit, out of sight from the potential victim. I could hear the clanging of the chain against the gate pole as he began to swing it shut. Fortunately, he left the car door wide open for me. So "like my pants were on fire" I jumped right on in! And to this day, I still get an unresponsive urge to "Jump and Jack" folks SUVs, as they leave the door open with the engine running while paying for their gas (see: Pay the Piper).

As I landed on the plaid cloth seats, I instantly could smell the stale cigarette smoke permeating the interior. After I slammed the door, "my plan" was to stomp on the brake, which releases the linkage, drop the gear shift down one click into reverse *and away I would go,* just like many times before...right?

Why the car did not move once I dropped it down one gear from park still eludes me to this day! I knew it was an automatic, I saw only two peddles on the floor as I jumped in! In a "life and death" situation, such as this, when I have made myself vulnerable to be *seriously hurt*, my mind reacts instinctively to find instant alternatives to what would normally be a "seemingly **hopeless** situation."

Unfortunately, this was *not* one of those times.

The movement I caught out of corner of my eye was kind of shocking because now the very aware customer was reacting like a super hero as he closed that ten foot space between us *in one* single leap! It was like a blur he did it so quick. But I did know one thing, though, and that is that I had just made a terrible mistake. **I forgot to lock the door** once I slammed it shut!

I hadn't planned on staying for dinner or anything and I wasn't even looking forward to educating him on how to get his car back. At this time I didn't even want to be in LA County! I quickly looked down to see what the problem was. The E-brake was off and I was looking at the gear shift indicator showing 'R' just as the door came open! Up to this point I was in full-on "escape mode" but I was finally able to switch gears. Only I was switching into "survival mode" *not reverse*!

Here is the part when I always wonder "just how bad I'm going to get hurt," if not killed! "***Repossession***" was the only word I was able to get in as I felt the hardest hit on the side of my head that I've ever felt!

"Like hell...my kid's in that car!" This was his war cry as he connected his closed fist to my head! Wham!

I saw a flash of light as my head was knocked onto the passenger window! Was this a trick? *I saw no kid in this car!* After hearing that, I almost felt deserving, as my head was getting slammed by his fists again and again. The angry Hispanic man was unloading onto me years of penile dysfunction, as he held onto the steering wheel with his left hand and threw a right cross over and over!

I did not see him put a child in there. Before I felt "totally" like a criminal, I blocked his punches the best I could (only having one hand) as I caught a glimpse into the back seat as my head was being jerked back and forth by his reoccurring blows.

There was no baby seat!

But under the unfortunate circumstances the negotiations had already been closed. I wasn't able to take a real good look into the back anyway, and it didn't really matter because I was *going down!* Then of course there was a new concern, **my glasses**. Yep, after that first blow to the left side of my head was delivered, my glasses were knocked clear off my head.

But first I had to get away from this, this psychopath. So as Brutus was catching his breath between punches, I reacted by leaning toward the passenger door, grabbed, and jerked up the door handle. In doing this my limp, beaten body just fell out onto the ground as the door opened. *I had found my freedom!* But this crazed individual was now "on a mission" to teach me a lesson!

As I began to crawl away from the passenger door, he leaned out the door and grabbed onto whatever he could to keep me as his "special guest" in this little House of Pain. Latching onto the tail end of my t-shirt, I felt myself being jerked back into the car. What's next? This guy had been watching way too many westerns! I wasn't going to stick around to find out how he wanted to relive his favorite episode of *Gunsmoke*.

But my shirt was too strong of material for me to try and "tear away from the situation." So his vengeance continued as he tried to reel me in by my shirt tail. Like a "dancer at Chippendales" I began to spin around, keeping myself out of his grasp and at the same time, I pulled each arm out of the shirt in such a "quick spinning fashion" that he should've tipped me a $20 for the performance. I was now out of his reach and he was left holding my shirt in his hand.

So with a frustrated look on his face, he snarled at me as I walked swiftly backwards in disbelief at what had just happened. "You're lucky I don't kill you and I will if I ever see you again!"

There was no need for me to stick around for anymore stimulating conversation, and there was nothing left to say. I wasn't going to say I was sorry...not me. He knew why I was there and I knew that **I had failed**. I was just so grateful to get away with only a couple scrapes and bruises (that was until I looked in the mirror). He had me in such shame to think that I would've even attempted to enter his car with his kid in there.

I looked into the backseat one more time, as I walked quickly "with my tail between my legs" and passed the rear of the vehicle. Still there was no sign of a kid...of any kind. Was this guy just trying to psyche himself up so he could put everything he had into defending his property? Whatever...

Shivering in the morning air, I quickly took "damage control" as I hurriedly stumbled away from the scene. My face instantly began to sting from the blows that, luckily, just grazed my face. It was the punches that *did connect* that left me dazed and throbbing! I was glad to just be walking away. And I didn't think that I was going to be making a return trip back here. After I saw the seriousness in his eyes as he growled out that threat, I didn't care if that unit and its driver went straight to hell. No, this is one of those repos (and there are only a couple) where I was going to admit "complete defeat."

But wait...I can't just walk away and leave my $140 glasses laying there on the ground now can I? Oh yeah! And he can keep the shirt. Every time he opens up his closet, he will remember if he made his car payment or not. There was no police report to file, or phone call to be made. I will just explain the whole situation on the message machine when I call in my nightly updates.

I did return, though, the next day after the customer left for work to look for my glasses, which I never found. And, in case you're wondering, yes, I did learn a big lesson here. This was, without a doubt my *very **last*** car jacking!

—Lefty

"Taze" the Puppet
Written and Experienced By: Michael S. Forcier

Our skip tracer Joan had a **"hot one"** for me. Mostly because I was the only one in the Long Beach area at the time. It was the month of September, 1989, and I was still driving Mr. J's big old Ford Dually.

God, did I learn to dislike that fat tank. Yeah, it was awesome when I first started to drive it back in '87. But now that I'd repossessed hundreds of cars by that time, I can tell you how inconvenient it was to try and squeeze that fat ass truck down driveway after driveway, leaving scrape marks, broken fences, and even pieces of the truck scattered all over Los Angeles.

It was tough to accept that it was gone, though. That is...once *it* got repossessed. Yep, the RO was my boss. And he got in a *little* over his head spending all that money I was making him. Like (Did I just start a sentence with 'like'? You can definitely tell that I'm from The Valley.) what happened to another company I worked for, when I was picking up three to five cars a night. The owner at the time made the unfortunate choice to start frequenting strip bars.

Once that repo order went out on my truck, it wasn't seen much at all. But after the bank put a $1,000 bounty on its hood, the boss (the RO) couldn't even trust his own employees. I remember doing stake-outs in it when I was the one being followed! Once the bank got back what was left of it, I'm sure the balance exceeded $10,000. No really...I tore those fenders completely off backing up alleys and driveways so many times, that all I could do from getting a ticket, was to keep mud flaps on it. The fiberglass wheel wells were peeled back so far on both sides, that you could see the side tool boxes. I received a couple Fix-It tickets for its unsafe condition.

But of course I continued to drive this truck under whatever the condition was. This was my first tow truck to use, and I drove it until the wheels literally fell off! That truck was so unique. I decided that since it was being used in the assault of folk's property, that this special truck from that point on would be known as the…urban assault vehicle (UAV).

I don't think you could comprehend how grateful I was after having my first two years in this business stealing cars without a tow truck. It was so frightening at times. I actually got sick to my stomach one time and puked onto the floor of some poor guy's Saab. That particular incident not only found me so scared that my knees shook so badly that I thought the whole car was shaking along with me. I was so pissed and frustrated because I could not find the stupid ignition for the life of me. **It was on the arm rest!**

In a few of these stories, you will see how taking a car with burglary tools really makes you appear as a burglar (see: LAPD Shift Change) and you even feel like one. I mean **really**, what would you think if you came out in the middle of the night to see a man in your car lying under the dash? That's when those "people skills" (or survival skills) really come into play!

At this time our four employee team was equipped with two-way radios. This was the second best piece of equipment next to "Go-Jaks." The cell phones at the time looked like they had just come off the set of *Combat*. So only the "rich and horrendous" had one.

Our skip tracer was getting very close to nailing the guy she radioed me about. Both of the other times I chased her "APBs" I only missed the guy by minutes. A good skip tracer will take their time when trying to corner these elusive characters, always handling the situations with "kid gloves," being very careful not to tip them off. Once they've been tipped off, you're not only back to "square one" but that unit gets buried so far that once it is found, there isn't much left but a frame in a South Central alley.

Her excitement was reassuring as I heard her voice come over the radio, "Come in Lefty," she spoke in a low and seductive tone.

"What do ya got?" I already knew that if Joan was on the radio, it could only mean one thing. Of course that is unless "Mr. J" got himself beat up again by another bunch of "Mountain Men" (see: Cold and Scared).

Her voice cut through, right after the connecting *bleep, bleep* of the two-way. "Remember the construction worker that you went to catch at the job site down in Laguna Niguel, only to have just missed him?"

Need she remind me…I wasted an hour and half drive to the most southern Orange County coast, just to have missed the perp by minutes. But I did try to curb my sarcasm, "Oh yeah, I think I remember that."

She continued, "Well, this time I got him a lot closer, and he's at a residence, doing a remodel in La Habra."

Still La Habra was a bit of a putt. But I'll take thirty miles on the 210 over fifty miles on the 405 any day! Joan loves to give me these locates. Mostly because I get them and **I never say no**. She also has been known to kick me down a few bucks for the tough ones. I also love the challenge in having such a high success rate.

I copied the address down clearly, having one too many "wasted efforts" from going to the wrong address and finding myself in many uncomfortable situations after trying to decipher my own "chicken scratch." After a short drive in the blue Ford Dually truck (that looked like a farm tractor) I had arrived in La Habra, a pretty city, one of those quaint old towns near the San Bernardino Mountains. After you make your way through the mile or so of Main Street, do you find yourself winding the residential streets up into the hills. That's where I found my address. A corner lot, sporting an older one story single family dwelling.

I glanced at the address on the curb as I quickly drove past. Remember this truck is easy to draw attention to, looking like it just came out of the *Road Warrior* movie. I quickly pulled around the corner and out of sight.

I radioed in to acknowledge the fact that I had arrived. "Yeah, I'm here," I already knew the drill once arriving at a location. "Our unit isn't showing in front, but there is a long driveway leading all the way to the back. I'll get right back to you on that. I'm leaving my radio in the truck." You can imagine how my cover has been blown in the past time, after time, by that annoying *"bleep, bleep"* of the two-way radio.

I left my truck unlocked, with the keys in the ignition. I think that anybody would be more afraid to even go **near that truck**, as scary as it looked, let alone **try and steal it!** As always, I needed to be ready to run back and jump in. And I didn't have time to fumble for an ignition key when I only have a small window of opportunity to get hooked up when every second counts.

As I walked back the two property lengths to the house, I was welcomed by the sound of a circular saw coming from in back of the residence. "Skaaawwwwwwww!" This is exactly the kind of thing I wanted to hear, for a number of reasons. To cover any noise I might make and, now that the guy is supposedly busy, I can "James Bond" my way back to the rear of the house to see if the 1986 Ford station wagon is back there.

Keeping my eyes trained on the house, so that I might spot someone before they spotted me, I started the careful walk down the driveway. You never know what or who you can run into at any time, so I always needed an immediate response ready once I got confronted. As I approached, I was able to make out the guitar sounds of what sounded like "Layla" by Derik and the Dominoes coming from in back of the house. Walking carefully down the driveway I noticed that it seemed a bit narrow, maybe *too narrow* for "The Tank" (my life's story with this truck). But fortunately it opened up into three or more, large car spaces back by the garage.

As I got closer to the end of the home, I could barely make out in the far parking space a light brown Ford station wagon.

That was it!

But it wasn't worth a trip back with the hook until I've at least made out the license plate. So standing with my back to the side of the house, I slowly peaked around the corner. I was lucky if this character didn't swap plates like most "Skips" do. Pulling back, I looked down at the clipboard at the area on the repo order for the plate. I knew that with all the "dain bramage" I suffered, I would only be able to remember the first two or three letters from the left, so that's what I read, "2GHY." A positive identification had been made.

I began to look back around the corner a little further, when I saw part of a large man in a t-shirt, *walking right toward me*! My instant reaction was to casually start walking back up the driveway and the thought of what I was going to say to him came right after it. You know that I cannot "burn" this account. Especially after all the work every one has put into it. So my plan was when "Jethro" came around the corner, I'll just go into "lost dog" mode. So I hunched over and, for added effect, I pulled my naked stump out from under my jacket. If the lost dog trick didn't work, maybe I can shift gears into "Retard Time." That one is a bit more difficult to pull off, but I've gotten away with it before.

Just as quickly as I heard the stomping of Jethro's boots coming toward the corner, did I hear them do an about face and go back. Whew! That was close.

Still taking in consideration that someone could be in the house, I ducked down below each of the three, three foot tall windowsills, as I scurried back up the driveway. As I got onto the street I turned and looked back, making the final decision if the fat ass Dually was going to fit up that driveway. And you know me, "where there's a will, there's a way."

In the position that Jethro had the wagon parked, I "should" be able to make one quick turn after rounding the corner, then slip my tow-sling right under his front bumper. Being a car and not a pick-up truck, I would not be able to use my "Quick Pins." "Quick Pins" are two, thick steel pins that are inserted into the lower boom, sticking up out of the bottom of the sling. When I'm able to use these, I can go up and around the bumper, not having to get out of my truck to use my tow chains in getting the vehicle up off the ground and into my possession.

I was going to have to hook up the old fashion way on this one. And have to physically get out of my truck, get under his vehicle, and hook not one, but both my tow hooks around each side of the front "A" frame! This complete procedure will be done while Jethro is making the decision, "Do I want to get stupid and assault this guy or do I cooperate?" That is the part of my job that keeps other repossessers changing carriers after only a short time in the field. What they fear most is what the enraged customer is capable of doing in his "thirty seconds of fame." I walked back to the truck and radioed into the office, "The unit is here and accessible. The only thing is, the RO is in back working by our unit." I gave Joan the full rundown.

She came right back with, "Okay, I've got a phone number going into the house. Let me see if I can "gag" him to the phone."

That was good enough for me. I would've preferred her talking the guy out of the car altogether. But you can't have everything. Besides, this guy is a big time skip, there must be "no contact made" whatsoever! That is, at least not until I secure possession of the unit.

Once back at the truck, I took each of the tow hooks off of the sling and laid them onto the bed for easy access. Also, it was so the chains didn't get "pinched in" just in case my angle is crooked once I make contact with the front of the Ford Wagon. I threw out of reach any items that could be used to help the RO damage my UAV, (*or me* for that matter). Once a person is confronted with losing one of their best assets to making a living, it's hard to picture the destructive things they will do in total desperation.

I climbed in and before I fired up the UAV, that "all too familiar" flash of fear came into my head of *what could happen*. But of course being a good repossesser, it's not what could happen, it's how do I handle it when Jethro grabs that circular saw and kindly offers to make me a paraplegic if I don't "back off" his ride!

I started up the truck and, before I dropped it into drive, I radioed in to Joan to check on that phone call. "Okay, where is our boy now?"

"I'm making the call now...stand by," she was right on top of it. Joan has been after this "goof" for some time now and was ready and eager as I.

I turned the UAV around and, just as I sat at the house before his, came that enthusiastic voice over the radio, "I got him on the phone now!"

I didn't even slow down as I continued looking in my mirror. I placed my stump onto the steering wheel and picked up my "customized hand controller" for the tow boom. I backed into the front of the narrow driveway unable to see a "light at the end of the tunnel." That's when the sick feeling of failure began to swell up in the pit of my stomach. Just like a lot of these narrow driveways, the chances of me fitting through were 50/50 and were diminishing by the second.

I slowed down just in time to find myself jammed between a fence post on my left and the god-awful sound of very thick bottle brush scraping into the paint of the UAV on my right. I wasn't going to make it!

Fortunately frustration overpowered my anger as I found myself "in this most unfortunate situation" one too many times with this fat ass truck. Like it was part of the "hooking-up process," I shoved the gear shift down into drive, unwedged myself, pulled out of the driveway, and around the corner. Only a miracle could've kept my display of "truck wedging" unnoticed by Jethro.

So I parked the truck and pressed the radio call button immediately. Instantly I heard the bleep-bleep of the radio followed by Joan's voice. "Did you get it?"

I didn't want to darken her spirits any, so instead of a failing "No," I answered with a possible plan "B." "Do you still have him on the phone?" I asked.

"No, but I can...what happened?" she asked in anticipation.

The driveway wasn't wide enough for the stupid truck. But I haven't seen him come flying outa there... yet. "I think we may have another chance at this." My repo skills came into play as I gave her the logistics of my planned suicide. "I heard the radio playing from inside our unit when I first identified it. So I think there's a good chance the keys are in the ignition. Let me know once you have him back on the phone and I'll make my move." I know this sounded a bit risky, but I had this "never give up" attitude when it came to this sort of situation. For the bank it's great, but for me…*it's very dangerous*.

Just like plan "A," only until she gets him away from our unit and on the phone in the house, can I make "my move." Placing the UAV back into drive, I drove down the opposing street and around the corner from the residence. This would be my safe haven for what I like to call a 911 repo. This is where I will leave the UAV. So after I "jack the car," obtaining possession, I can drive out of sight and as fast as I can get the car hooked up before the RO can run to my location. But it's important not to drive too far from the address and away from my truck, for a number of reasons. Usually two blocks is plenty. That is, unless the guy or gal (see: High Heeled Hitch Hiker) can do a twenty yard dash in 9.5 seconds!

I dropped the boom, leaving the keys in the ignition. Stuffing the folded repo order into my pocket, I thought of one more thing. I have this taser gun that I've fortunately never had to use. Just the fear that it generates by the three inch arc and the loud clak, clak, clak, the device can be very intimidating, to say the least. There have been quite a few times when being approached by a vicious dog, did I display *"THE ARC OF DEATH."* I quickly strapped on the holster that held the plastic gun, rolled up the windows, shut the door, grabbed my radio, and did my very own thirty yard dash to an adventure that was to be very surprising…to say the least!

I started out at my usual pace with the understanding that upon arriving onto the scene, not only will my heart be pumping all that blood to my brain, but my adrenalin will be on high alert right along with it.

Approaching the neighbor's house, I stopped and "cued" the radio, bleep, bleep. "Come in." I was panting as I spoke.

"Are you ready?" her response put me on edge.

For what? I thought to myself. That's one of the advantages that was passed on to me from some distant warrior relative. I can handle pretty much every curve ball that can be thrown. But once in a while, I find myself "biting off more than I can chew" and hopefully this won't be one of those times.

As I stood in front of the neighbor's bushes, I turned down the radio volume and responded, "Ten four." Just like "clock-work" the uneasiness came over me like a dark cloud. The *what-ifs* were all over me like I just stepped through a spider web. But knowing how to respond to it with action, I held the radio to my ear and waited for the "all-clear" signal. "Okay. He's on his way to the phone. I'll just cue the radio once I have him on the line."

The "what ifs" were replaced by a surge of adrenalin that would make a nun tweak-out. Then came the signal. Bleep, Bleep. Like out of a sling shot I instantly rounded the corner and headed down the driveway in "stealth mode." I ducked under the first window, while at the same time tried to listen for a voice. Then as I ducked under the second window, I heard Jethro for the first time. His voice was faint, but I assumed the low growling was his. Joan was doing what she does best by keeping him occupied.

The voice stopped just as I rounded the corner into the back. The commercial that was coming from the car's radio calmed me a bit as I knew that the keys had to be in the ignition. Better yet, Jethro must've disconnected the door buzzer, because he had the driver's door, wide open waiting for me! Yes...now I didn't have to chance opening a squeaky door.

That's when *my luck ran out* (not to mention my heart skipped a beat). Just as I moved up to the front of the unit, did I realize that, sure Joan had him on the phone, but the phone she had him on just happened to be ***IN THE GARAGE!***

There was no backing out now. It was hero time! I normally don't let fear cloud my judgment when it comes to split second decisions such as this, but the guy was *standing **right at the tailgate*** *of the station wagon!*

But I "went for it" anyway.

Just as I flew around the open driver's door, I heard his low voice stop in mid-sentence. Without even a glance in his direction, I jumped onto the worn fake leather seat. As I slid down onto the driver's seat, *I almost had a heart attack.* I felt the *"whole seat jump"* from underneath me accompanied by a frantic "yelp!" I saw out of the corner of my eye, as the light brown animal jumped out of the passenger's side. I had just sat on a rather large pit bull puppy! I don't know who was more scared, the four or five month old dog, or me.

Just as the dog was jumping out the passenger side window, I turned the ignition key over. As the engine fired up, I stomped onto the brake peddle and dropped the gear shift down into drive, the whole time expecting a sharp blow to my head...*or worse!* Fortunately the car was head out, making my escape that much easier. I jerked the car forward, forcing the driver's door to slam shut.

That's when Jethro made himself known. Not only did he have the car door open, but our hard working man, had the tail gate down as well! And this is where he made his grand entrance! Thud! The fear began to well up into my throat as I felt the back end of the wagon go down about six inches. This guys gotta be over 250 pounds!

"Oh shit," I thought to myself. I no longer had possession of the unit and was about to get my head caved-in, by one big pissed off construction worker! Just as I looked up into my mirror, I freaked as I saw this giant man crawling on all fours towards me, did I remember *my taser gun!*

Like we were now car pooling, I got to the end of the driveway, rounded the corner of the house, and pulled into the street. I found myself with just a *split second* before his big fist would be crushing my head! Just after I made the corner into the street, I freed my only hand from the steering wheel by sticking my stump between the bracing. As I reached down to my side to pull out *the equalizer*, I could hear his grunting and snorting as I was sure I was about to be blasted into the next county.

I whipped up the taser and pulled the trigger. *Clak, clak, clak*, the gun made its horrific sound! But it wasn't the sound of the gun that caught my attention. Amidst that annoying arcing did I hear a grown man shriek like a twelve year old little girl! *"Eeeek!"* I didn't know if there was a little girl hiding in the back seat along with the sleeping pit bull. In all the tension and drama, it took everything to keep me from *busting out laughing*.

"Please, don't use that thing on me!" This big giant burly construction worker had, right before my eyes, morphed into a very frightened "gay-boy."

Wow! One second I'm fearing for my life and the next I'm protecting my heterosexuality. The voice that came from the backseat was nothing at all that would fit the giant that had just come crawling up from the rear, ready to kill. I'm beginning to really like this taser gun. It's like a *Magic Wand*.

"I know I'm behind on my payments. I'll give you the car...J-just don't s-shock me with that th-thing!"

He was so cooperative that I was kind of suspicious. This giant man must've had a real "Rodney King Experience." I felt like the judge and the jury as I answered his plea, still holding the taser in his line of vision. I made it look like I had the gun do the talking, as he watched me *bob it around word for word*. It was kind of like the "puppet from Hell" as I used the gun to tease the poor guy. "Okay, here's what where going to do. Since we both don't want to see you crap your pants while you get the 400,000 watt attention getter, why don't we turn around, and let you get your stuff out...and maybe your dog will help you." My sarcasm was so unnecessary. But as that shriek was still echoing in my head, I just couldn't help it.

"Okay... but I only live a couple miles from here. If, if you would be so kind to let me unload the equipment I have occupying this space along with the other articles belonging to me, I would be truly indebted to you."

Who was this guy, a descendent of Shakespeare or something? I used *Taze Puppet's* eyes to look around the car and realized, there was no way that I was going to spend the rest of my evening writing up this pack-rats property. Taze shook out a response, "Okay, but I just want you to know that just in case you think that you're going to get over on me by calling out your mountain buddies, I will have LAPD on the phone the whole time." Little did he know that I had to call it in anyway.

Driving carefully with only my stump, so Taze could guard the prisoner, I watched as Jethro sat back. I found it safe to lay "Taze the Puppet" onto the seat. I picked up the radio and while I kept an eye on him, I pressed the "cue" button. Bleep, bleep. With my professional announcer voice I said, "Eagle to base." I might as well have some fun now that Jethro or "Jethra" or whoever this guy was in my back seat, that was no longer a threat.

"Go ahead," she was standing by waiting to see if I got possession of the unit.

I guess I wanted to see how far I could take this guy so I responded with, "Roger base, the eagle has found the nest and has laid the egg." I had to look down at the floor so that Jethra couldn't see me trying to control myself from busting out laughing. Might as well lay it on thick. "Yes base and we also have a 5-60 to go along with the 9-30." Now, she knows that there is someone else in the unit with me, because those numbers I just gave her *do not mean a god damn thing!*

"Ten four Eagle. Good work." I could tell by the tone in the response that she just got finished "picking herself up off the floor" after losing it herself.

—Lefty

Tommy's Lay Down
Written and experienced by: Michael S. Forcier

In the repo business, a "Lay Down" is normally a "volunteer" repossession when the customer hands over the delinquent vehicle. But not in this case though. The lay down I'm referring to in this case actually involves lying down.

I don't normally work on weekends, mostly because of all the drunk drivers and intoxicated customers. They never seem to act rationally when getting their car repossessed after they've had a few. So it's much safer staying off the streets on weekends. Besides, that is the only chance I have to get any *real* sleep.

The vehicle I received in my Thursday night's work was a 1988 Lincoln limo. The customer (it sounds funny calling them customers, when we are there to steal their livelihood, not serve them) fraudulently acquired this vehicle by falsifying income statements, which most likely wasn't his doing. Yes, the dealer that he leased the vehicle from has been known to do this before.

So what ends up happening is that the customer is completely unaware the new vehicle that he proudly is behind the wheel of, is on the hot list with the bank and is about to be repossessed without his knowledge. The problem with repossessing limos is that when they are finally out of their secured garage, they are always with a driver.

Another problem I have encountered with repossessing limos is that most companies own more than one, and their license plates are usually personal plates relating to the company and numbered #1, #2, and so forth. Now when one of the cars is about to get repossessed, they just leave that plate behind and put on another plate. This makes it very difficult to identify. That is unless the creative repossesser can get close enough to read the VIN off the lower edge of the windshield.

The bank, of course, had an address for the company. It was in the Wilshire District, west of downtown LA. Most of the buildings on Wilshire Boulevard are high rises and the vehicles, if they are even parked at the same location, are going to be *extremely* difficult to get a tow truck in and out with a stretch limousine on the hook. Winding its way around the tight corners of a parking structure is almost impossible. Fortunately, most were Ford/Lincoln Mercury products and I could "Slam Out" the ignitions (read: The Limo Chase).

Well Joan, our reliable skip tracer (who was still with us at this time) had a great plan for getting our limos out in the open to be preyed upon. This certain Lincoln limo was black in color. So she would call the dispatch office of the limo company and request a black Lincoln limo, along with as much detail associated to our unit as possible, to pick her up at a choice restaurant that we gave her, due to the fact that were no windows on the building. Now just in case they had more then one, each of us would take turns calling and requesting the same type of limo, matching as close to our description as possible on the same night, without sounding too obvious of course. We would set up pick up locations that were not too far from each other so that when our unit did show up, our truck would be "right on top of it."

As in most repossessions, the timing is very important. Mostly because there is only a small window of opportunity before you've got an extremely angry customer in your face, ready and willing to use force if necessary to keep from having his most valuable possession taken from him. Why we chose a restaurant without windows is obvious. Our plan involves the driver going into the restaurant to make contact with his party. This way he completely leaves the limo unattended. Even though he locks the vehicle up, as soon as he enters the building and that door closes behind him, it's all over but his "frantic phone call to the boss."

Our luck was with us in this particular situation. The dispatcher described our limo to a "T" when she told us what was going to be picking us up for *our anniversary night out.*

On a Saturday night the traffic in this part of LA is nuts! "To say the least." My directions were to park a block away from our favorite set-up restaurant, over on 3rd and Virgil. I arrived at my location and parked in a diagonal parking spot at an empty strip mall lot, waiting for the two-way radio call to "come and get it." There I sat for a half hour, just waiting for the whistle to blow and I'd be off to the "hook and book."

As an hour approached, I called Mr. J, my boss. After hearing the bleep, bleep of the talk button I said, "What's happening?"

Just like he had the radio up to his lips waiting for my call, he instantly responded, "We just spoke with their dispatcher and apparently our unit had another drop off in Echo Park, but it's on the way now. The fun should begin in less then fifteen minutes." This was the sound of Mr. J's "secret agent voice" whenever we were on a stakeout. At least he had a "lighter than usual" attitude. I got uncomfortable when repossessors get so wound up just before a big extraction. As you can tell from reading these stories, I had to have fun at this…always!

It wasn't two minutes, when in came the call, "This is it! The car has just pulled up in front of the building."

Finally the words came over the radio that I'd been patiently awaiting. I answered with my usual response, "Do the plates match?" Because it's my ass on the line if I drive off with the wrong limo on my hook (and yes, every repossesser has his "wrongful" stories) so I never take another person's word for it… if I can help it. I always verify by reading the VIN ASAP.

"It's our unit." The response came back just a bit too soon to satisfy. His voice continued, "As soon as he walks in the restaurant door start over here, I'll tell you when."

Thirty seconds passed, a minute, then five minutes. What's going on, I wondered? Did they jack this guy's car without a tow truck? Was contact made and the driver was talked into giving up the vehicle? Anything is possible with Mr. J in charge. As much as he tries to play by the rules, he does take a lot of risks that can put him in a lot of "painful situations." Take for instance, the time when he went alone up into the hills of San Dimas and got caught doing a repo by a group of angry mountain men. After one of them made a blasphemous statement regarding Mr. J's Jesus t-shirt, Mr. J stupidly pulled out his 400,000 watt taser gun and tased the big goof, not even thinking of the retaliation damage from the other two big guys. I picked him up from the emergency room the next day! His face was pulverized with a broken nose, fat lips, and his rib was fractured. His hair was still sticking straight out from when they used his own taser on him. I felt sorry for the guy, but lost respect for him at the same time. So who knew what was going on here at Ricardo's Mexican Food?

So I took it upon myself to go check out the situation. I always hated being the last to know. I drove past the location and observed the unit still in the driveway tail out, and yes, the plates did match. "What's the 411?" I radioed in.

"Unfortunately, our driver arrived with another person in the car and we're trying to figure out a way to get him to go inside also, but it's not happening."

That was the response that took the wind out of my sails. These things seldom go off as planned. I backed into an alley a block away off of Virgil, sat, and just waited another two minutes in silence. Then came the **new plan** over the radio, "The driver is back in the unit and they're backing out as we speak. I think they're headed toward downtown on 3rd. What's your location?"

Lucky me! Because I changed locations, the limo was coming right at me. "I'm all over it like a cheap suit," was my light hearted response.

Good repossessers never give up. That is, unless the dedication to the chase becomes damaging or life threatening (or there's a chance of burning it). And you know me; I live for this kind of drama. So now it was up to me!

Fortunately "my posse" was right behind me and with the two way radios, we all could stick close together and change positions when needed, so as not to tip off the limo driver. Unfortunately, only having one hand I found it very difficult to communicate on the radio and drive at the same time. Another thing that was different in this case was that there were two people in this unit. One paying attention to the road and the other "riding shot gun." Mr. J likes driving on the next street paralleling the street that chase is taking place on. But he had no idea of what was going on, or where to go, unless I was giving him a constant "play by play."

Considering my handicap, it was just a matter of a few blocks before Mr. J was of no help, but a hindrance with me having to report our limo's every move by having to key the radio, steer, and talk, all at the same time. If you were sitting next to me at a stoplight, what you would see was a long-haired guy in a leather jacket, leaning over, and talking to what looked like his crotch! The area we were in was just northwest of downtown LA and remember, *it's a Saturday night.* Can you just imagine for one second, just how many black Lincoln limos are on the streets at that time?

As we traveled up Vermont, I stayed a safe distance of four cars back. It was damn hard making all those lights with out losing him. On a number of occasions I had to pass the cars in front of me from the parking lane, just to not lose sight of my unit.

He turned on Beverly and immediately pulled over unexpectedly against the curb and stopped. Was I made? There was no place for me to pull over without being obvious, so I had to continue going another half block and, fortunately, found a parking space. I knew now that my tow boom was exposed, but how else was I going to not lose sight of this guy?

I watched in my mirror as his passenger exited the vehicle. I "cued" the radio, "I'm parked eastbound on Beverly just past of Vermont. The passenger has just exited the limo and our driver is pulling back into traffic. And as we speak, he is now traveling right past me…and here we go."

I turned my head to the right, just as the driver passed, so he could not see me talking on the radio. I let only one other vehicle get between us, and I took up the chase. Unfortunately the vehicle I let between us was not in as much of a hurry as my limo friend… and I lost him at the next light!

Tailgating the tortoise in front of me, I made a hole big enough for me to zip around him. Then, as I whipped my head back and forth so fast, I looked like I was off of the *Jacob's Ladder* movie, I checked for cross traffic as *I ran the light*!

Punching it for the next block, the limo came back into view. Well at least I hope it's my limo! By now I was coming up onto Rampart Boulevard and the busy intersection where everybody comes to eat at the "Original Tommy's Burger." Yes, everyone eats there, especially LAPD's finest. Tommy must give them a discount, due to how many officers frequent this fine scarfing establishment, and tonight was no exception.

There I was, calmly minding my own business, just going through the intersection like every one else when I noticed a couple of the uniformed officers, **with guns drawn**, walking into the traffic lanes against my green light!

Now in this part of LA this can happen at anytime, on any evening, especially with the amount of testosterone and zeal in the air, due to the amount of officers on the scene. But the deputies were not concerned in the least with any other vehicle that was coming in their direction. That's when, just as I got across the intersection, all three deputies simultaneously raised their weapons and pointed them right at my crazy long-haired head, as they stepped *right in front of my truck*!

Now I've been in a lot of frightening situations at this point in my illustrious career, and a lot of them actually involved LAPD officers pointing guns at me, but I was really caught off guard with this one. Looking like a dear in the headlights, I slammed on the brakes, threw Cindy into park, and put up my **"*Hand.*"**

Along with the usual, "let me see your other hand!" I heard, "Turn off the engine and with your hands in sight, slowly exit the vehicle…now!"

I was too shocked to even think clearly. Why was I being profiled in this manner? Naturally, I instinctively complied.

As the officer kindly opened my door for me and with a "9 MM" in my face, he spat out with onion breath, and of all the stupidest questions he could think of said, "Where's your other hand?"

"I'm a…"

He cut me off by grabbing me by the back of the neck. With a paralyzing grip, he jerked me out of driver's seat and pushed my face to the ground, while the other two officers still had their police issue 45 caliber guns trained at my head. "I'm going to ask you one more time, Where is the gun?" He snarled that gnarly Tommy's Burger breath in my ear (dude, lay off the onions).

"I d-do n-not have a gun… O-officer." You could hear the fear in my shaky response. Overzealous cops freak me out, almost as much as cracked out gangsters!

By now the deputy had me displayed face down in the middle of Beverly Boulevard, spread-eagle, my legs and my arms spread apart. You could tell this was going to be the high point for everyone's evening, who just happened to be eating at Tommy's that night. The flares were out and the traffic was being diverted away, while my trucks interior had the best cleaning it's ever had.

I had a good ten minutes to evaluate my situation as the asphalt was becoming part of my complexion. The cop was not talking to me, since I wouldn't disclose the location of "the gun." All I could come up with was that this was a *serious* case of mistaken identity. That's when, after the world had seen all the personal things I keep behind my seat, the officer came right out and said, "The driver of a limousine stopped and said he was being followed by a long-haired guy in a black tow truck, banishing a firearm."

I paused for a second before I spoke in my defense, as to not get abruptly interrupted again. Laying face down in the street now for as long as I have, I was able to find a way to assert myself. But instead the humiliation continued, as the words were deflected as I was forced in talking to the smelly oily asphalt, "I am an auto repossesser on a stakeout and the gentleman, that unfortunately for the both of us, lied to you about the gun was correct with the fact of being followed. The bank hired me to pick up the Lincoln. The repo order is on the passenger side of the front seat. And like I began to tell you before, I never, ever, have used or possessed a firearm...sir."

The whole one minute monologue was calmly delivered with my face stuck against the warm asphalt as my limbs were spread out in a very embarrassing position.

The deputy, shaking his head, walked over to the others, still reveling my lifestyle to the world, looked at them and in a sarcastic voice he *yelled out* in the direction of the now present thirty or forty witnesses, "Apparently the suspect...is not armed!"

There was this unnerving two second moment of silence. All at once, every cop on the scene just ***busted out laughing!***

But not me. I was so humiliated and pissed off, that I didn't even wait for that prick to tell me to get up. I just crawled to my feet and with my hurt pride, I hung my head sporting the road rash imprint and slowly dragged my feet over to my truck.

The side show was over. But few watched on as the "incredible shrinking one-armed man" picked up each of his life's possessions, placed them in the cab of his truck, and drove off into the night.

—Lefty

Glossary

Tap out: An expression used in wrestling, when an opponent taps his hand onto the mat once he wants to surrender or concede the match.
Key-way: The hole in which you insert a key.
Putting the ball back in his court: Terminology used when describing that it is now the other person's turn.
Ball out: Slang term used in describing *going full force* or trying as hard as you possibly can to accomplish something.
Man Power: An employment agency that hires unskilled laborers.
Tweekers: A slang term used to describe methamphetamine addicts.
Negative vibe: Short for vibration, as in "sensing bad energy."
Day shot: Repossession term to describe an address the bank has given to look for the collateral in the daylight hours.
Collateral: Used here as the unit or car I'm looking to repossess.
Unit: The car I'm looking to repossess.
Updates: The information I leave each morning on the repossession company's answering machine so they can inform the client of the progress that is being made on locating their collateral.
R.O.: The registered owner of the vehicle in question.
Jacking: A slang term used, as in "stealing."
Same ball park: Terminology used when describing that something is close to being correct. Used here as "not even in the same ball park."
Go Jacks: A brand name for two large four wheel skates or small dollies that are twenty-five pounds each and used to be placed under tires of immobile automobiles. Once they have been kicked down onto the large lever, they are pulled together, lifting the car up off of the ground, and then it can be rolled freely in any direction.
Quick pins: Two solid-steel pegs that are inserted into the bottom of a tow boom so that once the tow truck is backed up to a vehicle, the *quick pins*

will catch behind the bumper of the vehicle to be towed once the tow boom is lifted up.

Cindy: Name I gave my third tow truck.

Hookin' & bookin' (hook & book): Slang term used to describe fleeing the scene once a car has been repossessed.

"A" frame: The extended part of the frame of a front-wheel drive vehicle that holds the axle and the wheel.

Prey: The vehicle about to be repossessed.

Man hours: The time spent working.

Made: Found out, looked at, noticed, caught in the act.

Fam damily: Slang for "damn family."

Elephant in the living room: Unmistakable, very noticeable.

Fake check: Playing off or pretending to go to a different address to look at, just in case I was spotted looking at the correct address.

VIN: Vehicle Identification Number.

Ma & Pa Kettle: Two characters used in portraying a backwoods, hillbilly family in a 1970s movie.

Porch people: A slang term used in describing an under-privileged family.

Money pit: A slang term used in describing a house or vehicle that consumes an incredible amount of funds to keep it operable.

Cotter pin: A looped pin that is bent on one side to lock itself in place.

Hero: A term used in the repossession business to describe a third party who involves his services in helping the customer from not letting their car be repossessed.

Corn fed: A slang term used in describing a large man who is raised on a farm.

Paul Bunyan: A mythological woodsman who was one hundred feet tall.

Carney: A person who works at carnivals.

Neanderthal: Primitive man.

Repo logistics: Legal rules of repossession.

Playing hard ball: Being factual, serious, and firm.

Hooked up: Getting the tow hooks around the axle of the vehicle and lifting it off the ground, as in repossessed.

CJ: Los Angeles County Jail.

Crack head: One who smokes crack, usually the lowest and most desperate user in the drug world.

Tight wad: A miser who hordes his money.

Cut: The filler used to make drugs weigh more before they're sold on the streets.

Pimp out: Selling services for prostitution.

Devil's dick: A crack pipe.

Rolling: A: Slang term used when car dealers sell a car, as in, "He rolled it off the lot." B: When a police car arrives on a scene, as in, "The cops rolled on up."

"J" hook: The large metal hook at the end of the tow chain that hooks onto the axle of the vehicle to be towed, which happens to be shaped like a "J."

The Cindy Jerk: An expression Lefty uses to describe that his tow chain, or connection, was taught with the vehicle about to be towed.

Just like butta: A slang expression used to describe how easy something slides in or out.

Mumbly-peg: A game played with two kids slapping both hands together.

Booty: A Pirate's treasure.

Search & seizure: A legal term used when police look for, locate, and confiscate evidence.

Family jewels: Slang term used to describe the male genitals.

Playing possum: A phrase used to describe someone lying completely still.

Kujo: A rabid dog characterized in a Steven King novel.

Home boy or Homey: Slang term that started in the jail systems, describing another inmate from the same neighborhood.

Purple Heart: A hero's medal.

Grand Theft Auto: A popular video game.

Knee-Jerk reaction: An instant response.

Boat: Repo slang used to describe a rather large old car.

Caddy: A Cadillac automobile.

Tracking or dog running: Term used to describe a vehicle when it's being towed with the wheels partly turned so it would travel out of designated lane.

Swallowing crow: Eating my words, admitting mistake.

Boom: As in tow boom. The large metal sling that hangs off the back of a tow truck, which holds the towed vehicle.

Mr. Rogers: A child's television show host who speaks in a soft and timid tone of voice.

Ballsey: Slang term meaning "brave."

Crypt Keeper: A marionette puppet figured as a frightening skeleton with gray hair, the host for late-night horror movies in the 1980s.

Pan out: Term started by prospectors in the time of gold exploration to evaluate if there was gold in their pans to establish if the stream was worthwhile.

Blood money: Money given to a third party to reveal the location of the collateral or, in most cases, another family member.

Color of authority: Police code of ethics.

UAV: Urban Assault Vehicle, the name I gave to my second tow truck.

Wife beater T-shirt: A slang term used to describe a sleeveless, collarless, simple undershirt.

Gagging: Used here as in playing a gag on someone.

Back at the ranch: A term used to get back to what we were previously talking about.

Kid gloves: Term used in handling a situation in a sensitive manner.

SAG: Screen Actors Guild.

Jaws of life: A large hydraulic machine used to recover automobile accident victims by prying apart their wrecked cars to create an opening from which they can be extracted.

Stake out: Terminology used in the investigation field to describe when watching a certain subject.

Burned: Repossession terminology used to describe once we have been caught taking a car or even found out by the unsuspecting party in any way.

Unit: The vehicle about to be repossessed.

Aiding and abetting: A legal term used when one can be arrested for helping a known criminal in any way.

Skip tracer: An investigator who works with a repossession company who finds the people who skip out on their car payments.

Brutus: The big bully in the Popeye cartoon series.

Gunsmoke: An old 1960s western series.

Chippendales: A woman's entertainment club that features naked male dancers.

Taze: Abbreviation for using a taser.

Taser: A hand held electrical device that, with a 9 volt battery, produces an arc of wattage strong enough to knock a 300 lb man off his feet.

Combat: A 70s television series depicting WWII.

Rich & Horrendous: Mimicking 'Rich & Famous'

APB: Abbreviated police term meaning All Points Bulletin.

Perp: Abbreviated police term for perpetrator.

210: The northern route of three freeways used by LA commuters coming from eastern cities.

405: One of the busiest LA freeways that connects the San Fernando Valley all the way to Long Beach and beyond.

Chicken scratch: A slang term used to describe one's illegible handwriting.

Road Warrior: A 1980s adventure movie depicting survivors in a futuristic, rugged life style.

The hook: Repo term to describe the equipment used in the hooking up process of extracting the car.

Dain bramage: Brain Damage.

Jethro: One of the characters in a 1970s television series called the Beverly Hillbillies who was depicted to be large and uneducated.

Tweak-out: Slang term used in describing the actions of a methamphetamine speed user.

Rodney King: An LAPD arrestee who was caught on tape being "fazed" and beaten. The incident was the key issue that touched off the 1992 LA riots.

Lay Down: A volunteer repossession, when the customer gives the car up voluntarily.

Wrongful: As in wrongful repossessions, where the wrong car is repossessed.

Jack: Steal.

411: Information.

Riding Shotgun: A second passenger who is normally a lookout.

Play by play: Step-by-step directions.

Jacob's Ladder: A 1970s movie in which the star experienced gross hallucinations of creature's heads wobbling at a high rate of speed.